RHONDDA BOROUGH LIBRARIES

Lending Department.

1. This Book must be RETURNED WITHIN 21 DAYS FROM THE DATE OF ISSUE, but the loan may be renewed for a period of twenty one days on notice being given to the Local Librarian, and provided it is not required by another reader.

2. BORROWERS DETAINING BOOKS BEYOND THE AUTHORISED PERIOD will be liable to a charge of 3p. PER WEEK, or portion of a week, for each book so detained.

3. Borrowers must keep the books clean, and must not soil or deface them. Any damage done to a book will be charged for.

4. Books that have been exposed to any infectious disease must be handed to the Sanitary Inspector for disinfection. Penalty for non-compliance in this regulation is £2.

5. Borrowers are normally entitled to Four tickets :
   (a) Two General Tickets, available for all books.
   (b) Non-fiction (Not available for fiction).

   ssued to students on

   transferable

   reported without delay.

   refuse books, and may
   f borrowers who fail
   tions.

   VIES, A.L.A.,
   ough Librarian.

No. 946 PET   Class 515,554

RHONDDA BOROUGH LIBRARIES

This book is issued subject to our Rules and Regulations
and should be returned on or before the latest date entered below.

A Short History of
SPAIN

Sir Charles Petrie, Bt

C.B.E., F.R.Hist.S., Hon.D.Phil.(Valladolid),
Hon.Litt.D.(National University of Ireland), M.A.
(Oxon), Corresponding Member of the Royal
Spanish Academy of History, and of the Instituto
Fernando el Catolico of Zaragoza, President of the
Military History Society of Ireland

SIDGWICK & JACKSON
LONDON

946

ISBN 0 283 98100 8

Printed in Great Britain by
The Garden City Press Limited
Letchworth, Hertfordshire SG6 1JS
for Sidgwick and Jackson Limited
1 Tavistock Chambers, Bloomsbury Way
London, WC1A 2SG

Contents

Introduction   7

Important dates in Spanish History   13

1   The Classical and Medieval Periods   15

2   Spain as a Great Power, 1492–1808   31

3   Spain as a Great Power, 1492–1808 (continued)   47

4   The Last of Old Spain   63

5   Revolution and Restoration   80

6   The Directory and the Second Republic   95

7   The Civil War and the Franco Régime   109

8   The Spanish Genius   117

    Short Bibliography   123

    Index   124

List of Illustrations

facing page

1. Charles V — 32
   (*Radio Times Hulton Picture Library*)
2. Philip II — 32
   (*Radio Times Hulton Picture Library*)
3. Cervantes — 32
4. Charles III — 33
   (*Radio Times Hulton Picture Library*)
5. Alfonso XIII and Primo de Rivera — 33
   (*Radio Times Hulton Picture Library*)
6. General Franco and H.R.H. Don Juan Carlos — 33
   (*Associated Press*)

between pages

7. Interior of the mosque at Cordova — 64–5
   (*Paul Elek Ltd.*)
8. The Roman aqueduct at Segovia
   (*Radio Times Hulton Picture Library*)
9. The Battle of Lepanto
   (*National Maritime Museum, Greenwich*)
10. Avila
    (*Paul Popper*)
11. The Escorial
    (*Radio Times Hulton Picture Library*)

facing page

12. Valle de los Caidos — 96
    (*Paul Popper*)
13. Street scene in modern Madrid — 97
    (*Paul Popper*)

Introduction

The subject of this book is the study of a great civilization. It is the story of the influence which Spain has exerted in world history, first in medieval Europe, when she drove the Moslem invader slowly back, and then in America, when she colonized the greater part of a continent, without for a moment abandoning her traditional policy as the champion of Christendom against the infidel. It is possible to distinguish five main periods in Spanish history: first of all, the contest with Islam in the Peninsula itself, which occupied eight centuries of Spain's existence, and was the capital fact of it; then her discovery and conquest of the New World; next the establishment of the absolute monarchy, and the struggle against the Reformation; then her efforts to remain a great power; and finally her eclipse in the nineteenth century and present *renaissance*.

The common mistake made by British and American historians in dealing with Spain is to regard her as a world apart. They fail to depict Spanish events against their European background, and thus miss their significance, with the result that the British reader in particular is too often accustomed to regard Spain from the point of view of his Elizabethan forefathers. For two hundred and fifty years, that is to say from the death of Mary Tudor to the outbreak of the Peninsular War, England was intermittently at war with Spain, and the passions which were aroused during that contest have unfortunately been only too often reflected in the pages of British historians. The result has

been that the ordinary educated Anglo-Saxon on both
sides of the Atlantic still reads Spanish history with all the
prejudices of his ancestors. The propaganda that attracted
recruits to the colours in the days of the Armada still per-
meates the textbooks. The north American is in an even
worse plight, for he fought the Spaniards as recently as
1898, and it would be idle to deny that the bitter feelings
which that conflict engendered are wholly dead, at any
rate among the older generation.

For many people, therefore, in the days of her greatness
Spain was the embodiment of all that is evil; a power
which strove to suppress civil and religious liberty throughout the world, and was herself sunk in ignorance and
superstition. The novelist completed what the historian
began, and the Spaniards portrayed by such writers as
Charles Kingsley have been accepted as the normal type of
their fellow-countrymen.

The decline of Spanish power was described as the
inevitable consequence of the policy which had been
pursued in the sixteenth and seventeenth centuries, and
was generally treated as just retribution. It was not under-
stood that what had exhausted the nation's strength was the
simultaneous colonization of America and the struggle
against the Turks, and it was assumed, rather than proved,
that a misguided people had met a fate to which they had
been doomed from the beginning.

Above all no allowance was made for the economic
difficulties of Spain at this period, or for the effects of
inflation, which we are better able to understand today.
The discovery of America, and the importation into
Europe of precious metals in quantities previously unknown, caused a fall in the value of money, and a conse-
quent rise in prices: Spain, the possessor of the Indies, was
actually the first and the most seriously affected by this
development. If too much attention is perhaps paid to
economic history today, too little was certainly given to it
in the past, and for this reason, too, Spain has not re-

ceived a fair deal at the hands of more than one Anglo-Saxon historian. In her Golden Age she is shown as arrogant and intolerant, and when, in her decline, she was struggling to remain a great power, she is dismissed with a sneer as a beggar apeing the state of his betters. As for her history since the Napoleonic invasion which set her back for many years, it is invariably ignored save for the part which the British army played in resisting it, and nineteenth-century Spain is quoted as an excellent example of a nation that has had its day, and is scarcely worth a passing reference.

How those who adopted this standpoint reconciled it with the facts of Spanish civilization it is difficult to say. The people who were steeped in ignorance and bestiality produced Velázquez, Murillo, and Goya; Lope de Vega, Cervantes, and Calderón. Their architects designed the cathedrals of Burgos, Toledo, and Seville, not to mention the Escorial, and covered the New World with buildings that are among its most treasured possessions at the present time. For a hundred and fifty years, from the time of Gonzalo de Córdoba to the battle of Rocroy, the Spanish infantry were invincible, while Spanish sailors were revealing the secrets of the seven seas. Nor was this all, for America was being explored and colonized, and in the whole of recorded history there have been no feats to surpass those of the *conquistadores*. In the fuller knowledge and greater impartiality of today it must be admitted that the Anglo-Saxon presentation of Spanish history has too often been unjust.

The corollary of this persistent denigration of the Spaniard was the exaltation of his enemy, the Moor. The Mussulman who had conquered the Peninsula became the very pattern of chivalry, and the civilization of Cordova and Granada was contrasted with the alleged savagery of the Christian Reconquest. Those who took this line never stopped to enquire why, if this civilization was purely Mussulman, the Arab elsewhere should have remained in the most profound ignorance. The overthrow of Spanish Islam was written down as a definite calamity, and one from which unhappy Spain has never really recovered. The anarchy which was continually breaking out even in the heyday of Ommeyad power, and the ferocity which marked the rule of the various Arab dynasties, were glossed over or altogether ignored, and a picture was painted which bore but a scanty resemblance to the truth. We must be careful not to allow the romance of Mussulman Spain to blind us to the reality, which is that such of it as is worthy of praise was in fact Spanish.

The work of the Spaniards in America has likewise been far too harshly judged, and the civilization of their predecessors there unduly praised. The Incas were a case in point. Sometimes they were represented as the type of a good savage, full of innocence and virtue, such as would have been dear to the heart of Rousseau; sometimes as the heirs of a great civilization wantonly blotted out by the barbarism of the *conquistadores*. The truth is that what Spain set up was vastly superior to what she pulled down, and it is a mistake to allow our natural horror at the methods of the *conquistadores* (who were no more brutal than their English contemporaries) to blind us to their achievements, for they brought two-thirds of the American continent within the sphere of European culture.

Nor was Spanish rule in the New World the grinding tyranny that it is so often described as in British and North American textbooks; if such had been the case it would not have taken Miranda, Bolivar, San Martín, and Sucre so many years to sever the connection with Madrid. The contest which resulted in the independence of Spanish America was a civil war, in which the side opposed to the continuance of Spanish government was victorious after a long struggle: relatively few native Spaniards took part in the war, which was really one between the colonists themselves.

In the pages which follow it has been my endeavour to

place such events in their correct perspective, and in so doing not only to narrate the history of Spain, but also to show how much that great country has contributed to the common stock of our civilization.

CHARLES PETRIE

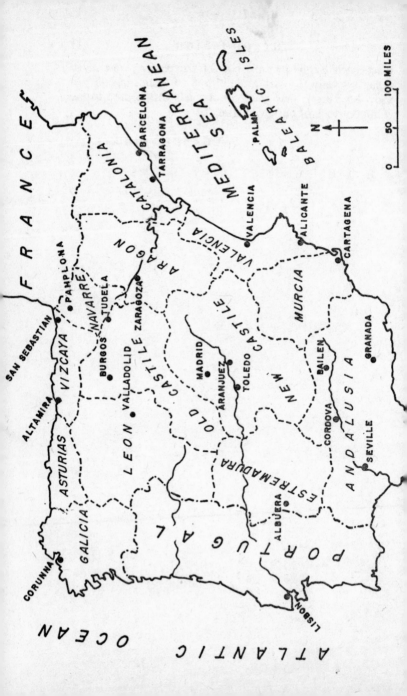

Important Dates in Spanish History

B.C.
(about 500) Carthaginian invasion
   217 Romans invade Spain
   133 Surrender of Numantia

A.D.
   409 Barbarians enter Spain
   415 Visigothic kingdom established
   711 Arrival of the Arabs
   929 Caliphate established at Cordova
1031 Fall of the Cordovan Caliphate
1085 Alfonso VI captures Toledo
1212 Battle of Las Navas de Tolosa
1248 Ferdinand III captures Seville
1492 Capture of Granada. Expulsion of the Jews
       Discovery of America
1504 Conquest of Naples
1512 Annexation of Navarre
1521 Battle of Villalar
1525 Battle of Pavia
1568 Moorish Revolt
1571 Battle of Lepanto
1572 Revolt of the Netherlands begins
1580 Conquest of Portugal
1609 Expulsion of the Moriscoes
1640 Portugal becomes independent
1643 Battle of Rocroy
1701 War of the Spanish Succession begins
1713 Treaty of Utrecht

1767 Expulsion of the Jesuits
1805 Battle of Trafalgar
1808 French invade Spain
1810 Revolt in Spanish America begins
1812 Constitution of Cadiz
1833–1839 Carlist War
1873 First Republic established
1875 Restoration of the Monarchy
1895 Insurrection in Cuba
1898 War with the United States
1923–1930 Directory
1931 Second Republic established
1936–1939 Civil War
1939 General Franco becomes Head of State
1969 Prince Juan Carlos of Bourbon nominated as future King of Spain

CHAPTER ONE

The Classical and Medieval Periods

The history of Spain dates a long way back, as far, in fact, as the prehistoric caves at Altamira, some eighteen miles from Santillana in the north-west, and at Nerpio in the province of Albacete in the south-east clearly prove. The former lie nearly 900 feet below the surface, and were not discovered until 1868: some of the wall paintings are estimated to be from 20,000 to 25,000 years old, and belong to the last Ice Age, others to the Stone Age. The Nerpio caves are a more recent discovery, for the real exploration of the site and recording of the paintings did not begin until round about 1960: the age of these paintings is generally considered to be mesolithic, that is to say they date from the period between the Old and the New Stone Age.

Little is known with any certainty about the early inhabitants of Spain, for although Hesiod mentions the country in the eighth century B.C. it was not until considerably later that the Greek writers began to refer to it in any detail. By this time the Peninsula was divided between the Celts and those who had preceded them; to the latter were given the name of Iberian, a term first employed by the Greek traveller Scylax in the sixth century. The Celts had recently invaded Spain from the north. It is impossible to do more than hazard a guess at the line of division between these two peoples, but it is probable that the region next to the Pyrenees, the Mediterranean coast, and part of the south were inhabited largely by the Iberians; that Galicia and Portugal were in the occupation of the Celts; and that the rest of the Peninsula was in the hands of a mixed race, whom ancient writers called the Celtiberi. The civilization of all was rudimentary, except on the east coast, where contact with the Phoenicians and Greeks had done something to raise the level.

The Phoenicians and the Greeks

Reliable tradition speaks of the foundation of a Phoenician colony at Cadiz in the eleventh century B.C., but the information collected by the Phoenicians has unfortunately only reached the modern world at second-hand. They established themselves chiefly in Andalusia and Murcia, as well as in the Balearic Islands, and they made the first notable contribution to Spanish civilization. They introduced money, which had hitherto been unknown, and they developed the mineral resources. After the Phoenicians came the Greeks, and the rivalry between the two was unending. The Greeks turned their attention chiefly to Valencia and Catalonia, and their principal settlements were Emporion (in the province of Gerona), Hemeroscopion (in the province of Valencia), and Dianium, as Denia was then called. They, too, brought Spain into touch with the culture of the eastern Mediterranean, and many traces of their influence have been discovered, notably the statue called 'The Lady of Elche' because it was found in that place in the province of Alicante. It must, however, be observed that both Phoenicians and Greeks were activated solely by commercial motives in going to the Peninsula, and they made no attempt to conquer the interior.

As Tyre and Sidon began to decline their place in the Mediterranean was taken by Carthage, a Tyrian colony on the north coast of Africa. The Carthaginians gained possession of some of the Balearic Islands at an early date, but it was not until the sixth century B.C. that they began to settle on the mainland. The occasion for their doing so was that they were called in by the Phoenicians of Cadiz to assist them against the neighbouring Iberian tribes. The citizens of Cadiz soon discovered that they had a master in their new ally, for the Carthaginians took full advantage of the opportunity to bring the various Phoenician colonies under their own rule, and also to commence the conquest of the whole Peninsula. This task was carried out by three generals of the Carthaginian family of Barca, namely Hamilcar, Hasdrubal, and Hannibal. At the height of her power Carthage dominated all Spain as far as the Douro and the Ebro, and she was also in possession of the Balearic Islands. The capital was New Carthage (Cartagena), which served, too, as the commercial centre of the whole country. The Carthaginians did much to develop Spain by building cities and roads; but save in a few places, notably the Balearic island of Ibiza, the remains of their rule are scanty, for the subsequent Roman domination was much more complete.

Coming of the Romans

The successes of the Carthaginians at length roused the jealousy of the Romans, who were at that time beginning to extend their power to the west. Accordingly, a treaty was made between the two peoples about the year 228 B.C., by which the Ebro was fixed as the line of division between their respective spheres of influence. This proved to be a mere truce, and Spain soon had her first experience of becoming involved in world politics. The town of Saguntum, although on the Carthaginian side of the Ebro, was under Roman protection, and its capture by Hannibal in 219 was the immediate cause of the Second Punic War. In the course of this contest the Carthaginians were finally driven out of the Peninsula, but it was not for many years that the Romans gained effective possession of more than the south. Nearly two centuries elapsed before Spain was completely conquered, and the tribes in the north and north-west, who had never submitted to Carthage, confessed themselves beaten. The Celtiberi were subdued by the elder Cato in 195, but the work had to be done again by Tiberius Gracchus in 179. The various tribes who inhabited what is now Portugal found a leader in Viriathus, and they only submitted in 137 to D. Junius Brutus, who penetrated as far as Galicia. In reality it was not until the capture of Numantia by Scipio Africanus the younger in 133 that the centre of Spain became definitely Roman. Later, Julius Caesar conquered the tribes north of the Tagus, and under Augustus (27 B.C. to A.D. 14) the subjugation of the country was completed by a successful campaign in Asturias. The trouble experienced by the Romans in their pacification of the Peninsula was in no small measure due to the fact that the Spaniards were already showing a marked aptitude for guerilla warfare, and it was their skill in this that time after time impeded the advance of the legions.

Roman Spain

As early as the end of the Second Punic War the Romans had divided Spain into two provinces, Hispania Citerior and Hispania Ulterior, with the Ebro as the boundary between them.

Augustus made a new division of the country, and formed three provinces namely Tarraconensis, Baetica, and Lusitania. The first of these, with its capital at Tarraco (Tarragona), was by far the largest, and included the north, west, and centre of the Peninsula. Baetica, which derived its name from the River Baetica (Guadalquiver), had the Anas (Guadiana) for its boundary on the north and west, and a line drawn from that river to the promontory Charidemum (Capo de Gata) on the east. Lusitania roughly corresponded in extent with modern Portugal. The basis of Roman rule was the town, and although at first there were slight differences of organization between towns of the Roman and of the native type, these disappeared when Vespasian (68–79), and, later, Caracalla (211–217) widely extended the privilege of Roman citizenship.

The inhabitants of each *municipium* were divided into residents (*cives*), temporary residents (*incolae*), and what may be termed the floating population (*hospites* or *adventores*). The first two classes formed a *populus*, which for certain purposes constituted a popular assembly. Until the second century A.D. this body elected the higher magistrates in a form similar to that used in Spain until very recent times for the election of town councillors. It also discussed at its meetings the general interests of the town, and passed any resolutions that it deemed necessary. The municipal magistrates were four in number, namely two *duumviri* and two *aediles*. The latter were responsible for such services as the policing of the town, while the former fulfilled administrative and judicial functions. Those in charge of the town's finances were called *quaestores* and those whose duty it was to prepare the electoral rolls and take the census were known as *quinquennales*; in addition there was a town council (*curia*) but its members were nominated by the magistrates, not elected by the people. The villages were largely dependent upon the towns, though they had their own assemblies. Once a year the Roman citizens in each province met to celebrate religious festivals, and when these were at an end those present resolved themselves into a *concilium* of which the principal duty was to approve or censure the acts of the governor, and if necessary to report him to the central government.

The Roman municipal system has left its mark upon the Peninsula to this day, for the vigorous town life of Spain has been one of the most remarkable features of her history. When the Spaniards colonized America they did so by and through the towns, and in much the same way as the Romans had done in Spain itself. Nor is the survival of this influence surprising when the intense Romanization of the country is taken into account. By the end of the first century A.D. the greater part of the native population had conformed to the civilization of their conquerors, and the culture of Rome naturally spread to the interior from the south, which had already been in contact with the Phoenicians and Carthaginians. In some ways Spain became the most Roman of all the provinces, as her contribution to the Empire amply proves. The Emperors Vespasian (68–79), Titus (79–81), Nerva (96–98), Trajan (98–117), Hadrian (117–38), Marcus Aurelius (161–80), and Theodosius (379–95) were all Spaniards, while of the great writers Seneca and Lucan came from Cordova, Quintillian from Calahorra, Martial from Calatayud, while Columella and Pomponius Mela were both Andalusians. The population of Spain during the reign of Augustus has been estimated at seven or eight million, and it increased during the long centuries of peace which followed. Domitian (81–96) reduced the garrison to a single legion, the Seventh Gemina, and a few auxiliaries, and at that strength it remained until the time of Diocletian (184–305).

Spread of Christianity

During the centuries that Spain was subject to Roman domination Christianity was implanted in the Peninsula. It is said to have been preached there by St Paul himself, and however that may be, by the third century there were already numerous Christian communities in the country. Spain provided its quota of martyrs in the days of persecution, and their blood duly proved to be the seed of the Church. As soon as official recognition was given to the new faith the number of proselytes grew apace, and the ecclesiastical organization of the Peninsula was completed. Various councils were held, and even thus early the Spanish Church was distinguished for the rigidity of its ideas and the orthodoxy of its doctrines.

In spite of the growing weakness of the Roman Empire and the irruptions of the barbarians into many of its provinces, it was not until the beginning of the fifth century that Spain again experienced invasion, although there had already been raids at various points along the coast. The first invaders to arrive were the central European tribes of the Suevi, Vandals and Alani, who entered the country in 409, and soon made themselves masters of the modern Galicia, Portugal and Andalusia. Three years later the Visigoths penetrated into Catalonia, and it was not long before they were at war with those who had preceded them. The Alani were politically annihilated, and the Vandals were driven across to Africa in 429, but it was not until 585 that the Suevian kingdom in Galicia was finally conquered.

The Visigoths

The Visigoths remained in control of Spain for three hundred years but they never succeeded in establishing themselves as the Franks did in contemporary Gaul. One reason for this was the extinction of their royal family, the Balts; for as soon as it became necessary to choose a monarch from the ranks of the nobility every ambitious duke or count could aspire to the throne. Each election was fiercely contested, and the defeated candidates at once began to conspire against their successful rival. Where no one had a prescriptive right to the crown the temptation to seize it by force was inevitable. In these circumstances it is hardly surprising that of the twenty-three Visigothic monarchs after the old line had come to an end no less than nine were deposed, and of these seven were murdered by their successors. The average length of their reign was less than eight years, and only in eight instances did a son succeed his father on the throne. There was but a single case of grandfather, father, and son following each other in undisputed succession.

A further weakness of the Visigothic regime was the gulf which existed between the conquerors and the mass of the population. In Gaul the Franks and the Provincials soon coalesced into one nation, but no such easy union was possible in Spain, because the great barrier of religion lay between the conquerors and the conquered. The Visigoths were Arian, who held to a heretical form of Christianity which their ancestors beyond the Danube had adopted in the fourth century: the Spaniards, on the other hand, were almost to a man fanatically orthodox. The Visigoths formed a religious community of their own, and their monarchs were thus unable to utilize the native episcopate for their own purposes in the way that the Merovingians were doing in France. As a result the Spaniards hated their conquerors both as barbarians and as heretics, and were quite willing to aid their enemies, particularly the east Romans and the Franks. While the Visigoths remained Arian no Spaniard was raised to power, and it was not until their conversion at the end of the sixth century that Roman names are found among those holding high office. Thus for the first hundred and twenty years of the Visigothic monarchy in Spain, that is to say during its formative period, the dominant race was completely estranged from its subjects.

The Visigothic kingdom consisted, then, of a servile population of Hispano-Roman origin, held down by a sprinkling of Gothic men-at-arms, each bound by oath to follow some great noble, who considered himself the equal of the king, and only vouchsafed him the barest homage. The history of Spain during this period is a record of civil war, suspended from time to time by the accession to the throne of some ruler who managed to preserve order while he lived. In the middle of the sixth century Justinian I (527–65) took advantage of the chaos in the Peninsula to attempt to reconquer it for the Roman Empire, and his generals rapidly subdued Andalusia. His successors at Constantinople, however, were too weak to carry on his work; but all the same, the east Romans remained in possession of Cordova and Granada for twenty years, and it was not until another fifty had elapsed that they were finally ejected from the towns on the coast.

In 587 King Reccared I embraced Catholicism, and his example was followed by the mass of the Visigoths, so that in a few years Arianism was a thing of the past. Unfortunately, one of the consequences of this conversion was excessively to increase the power of the Church, and there was actually a clerical majority in the National Council. After the death of Reccared I the history of the Visigoths becomes very obscure, and several of their monarchs appear to have been puppets of the clergy. The only capable sovereigns were the aged Chundaswinth (641–52) and his son Reccaswinth (652–72), but after them the kingdom began to decline rapidly. Of the later kings little is known except their names; while concerning the last of all, Roderic, we have no facts, only his name and a few exceedingly rare coins, though legend has been extremely busy with him and his alleged exploits.

The Arab Invasion

The closing decade of the seventh and the opening of the eighth century had witnessed the rapid expansion of Islam in north Africa, and the only place of importance in Christian hands was Ceuta, which still acknowledged the Emperor at Constantinople. The story that the governor of this place, one Julian, induced the Arabs to invade Spain in revenge for the seduction of his daughter by Roderic is a pure myth, though it is by no means impossible that the Byzantine exarch of this African port may have hoped that the diversion of Moslem energies into the Peninsula would relieve the pressure upon his own garrison. In 710 there was an Arab raid (clearly a reconnoitring expedition) on the coast of Andalusia, and in the following year the Moslems landed in force under the command of Tarik. Roderic appears to have marched south from Toledo, the Visigothic capital, to meet the invaders, and was routed in a battle that took place on the banks of the Barbate, near that river's junction with the Lake of La Janda. The Visigothic monarch was either killed in action or in the subsequent pursuit, and so little resistance did Spain make to the victorious Arabs that within two years the only district which had not submitted to them was the mountainous coast of the Bay of Biscay. So fell the Visigothic kingdom, and it is safe to assert that if it had not become a prey to the Arabs from the south it would before long have been conquered by the Franks from the north, for it had no real roots in the country.

The Arabs, or Moors as they are more often called, remained in the Peninsula until the conquest of Granada by Ferdinand and Isabella in 1492, and they left their mark permanently upon the Spanish character. Their rule was a school of anarchy, of which the teaching has unfortunately never been forgotten. Not only were the original invaders divided among themselves by differences which dated from pre-Islamic times, but they were continually being reinforced by Moors and Berbers, who introduced fresh centrifugal tendencies. In addition, there were the complications, common to the whole Moslem world, which resulted from the dispossession of the Ommeyad dynasty of the Caliphate in 750. The period of Arab rule in Spain, like the Visigothic, was marked by repeated civil wars, only suspended when some ruler strong enough to impose his will upon his rivals made his appearance. That swing of the pendulum between the extremes of authority and licence, so characteristic of Spanish and Spanish-American history, is due to Arab influence. On the other hand, there was a standard of civilization unknown to contemporary Christian Europe, though the basis of it was Roman. The architecture of the celebrated mosque at Cordova is an excellent example of the many influences at work in Moslem Spain. From the Arab, too, the Spaniard acquired a realism that at times has come very near to fatalism.

The Visigothic kingdom had been conquered in the name of the Caliph, but Damascus was far from Spain, where the governors were a law unto themselves. In the first forty years of Moslem rule in the Peninsula there were no less than twenty viceroys, of whom Musa was the earliest and the most notable, and of these seven came to a violent end. Nevertheless, the work of conquest went on, and the Arab hosts crossed the Pyrenees. Nismes, Carcassonne, and all Provence up to the Rhône were added to the dominions of the Caliph. In 732 it was decided to conquer Aquitaine, and a large Moslem army captured Bordeaux on its way north. At Poitiers the Franks under Charles Martel met the invaders, and decisively routed them in the great battle, one of the most decisive in history, falsely called that of Tours. It was in reference to this contest that Gibbon wrote, if Charles Martel had been defeated, "Perhaps the interpretation of the Koran would now be taught in the schools of Oxford, and her pulpits might demonstrate to a circumcised people the sanctity and truth of the revelation of Mohammed." However that may be, the further penetration of western Europe by the Arabs came to an end, although they retained a foothold in the south of France for many years.

The Cordovan Caliphate

The overthrow of the Ommeyad dynasty and its replacement by the Abbasid resulted in the establishment of Spanish independence, for a scion of the dethroned line, Abderrahman, fled to the Peninsula, where he founded an emirate, with its capital at Cordova. In 929 the greatest of his successors, Abderrahman III, assumed the title of Caliph, and the two generations which followed this event marked the golden age of Moslem rule. Cordova kept alight the torch of civilization which had been extinguished elsewhere, while the armies and fleets of its masters both secured the coasts of Spain from attack, and enabled Spanish merchants to trade freely with all the ports of the Mediterranean. At this time, too, Arab rule was still tolerant, and there were many conversions to Islam among the Christian population as well as intermarriage between the two races. It is true that the regime was neither more nor less than an Oriental despotism, in which the citizens were at all times subject to the caprice of their ruler, but in the dark of tenth-century Europe the comparative peace and culture of the Ommeyad Caliphate of Cordova formed an oasis which its subjects had no desire to leave. Gradually the power of the Caliphs grew less, while that of their viziers increased, and it was the greatest of these, Almansur, who sacked Santiago de Compostela. In 1031 the Caliphate itself collapsed, and Moslem Spain was plunged into anarchy.

Christian Reaction

Meanwhile, although the Visigoths had put up so futile a resistance at the time of the Arab invasion, the more resolute of them refused to accept the rule of the Crescent, and in the mountains of the north-west they established a state of their own, of which one Pelayo was chosen as monarch. At first their new kingdom was little more than a collection of fugitives, but as the Moslem tide receded it began to enlarge its boundaries. Even at this early date those centrifugal forces, which have always been so strong in the Peninsula, came into play, and within the still narrow limits of Christian Spain there grew up the kingdoms of Portugal, León, Castille, Navarre, and Aragón, and the county of Barcelona. It is true that on several occasions more than one of those crowns was worn by the same sovereign, but disputed successions were frequent, and the energy that would better have been devoted to the reconquest of Spain from the infidel was too often dissipated in fratricidal strife. Nevertheless, the frontiers of Islam steadily receded, for there was more civil war among the Moslems than among the Christians, and in 1065 Alfonso VI of Castille captured Toledo, the old Visigothic capital.

This struggle against the Moslems lasted for over seven centuries, and it made a lasting impressions upon the Spanish character, for it was a clash between two opposing and irreconcilable civilizations. Attractive as were the splendours of the Cordovan Caliphate, they represented only an interval in the history of Spain, for in the main they belong rather to the annals of Islam, and the development of the national culture took place in the mountains of Asturias rather than upon the banks of the Guadalquivir. At the same time it is a mistake, as has been shown, to suppose that the feeling between Christian and Moslem was always one of animosity. What exacerbated tempers on both sides were the consequences of the fall of Toledo. Prior to that event the population of Islamic Spain had been mainly Arab, but the progress of Alfonso VI so alarmed the rulers of the petty kingdoms which had grown up on the ruins of the Cordovan Caliphate that they invited Moors and Berbers from north Africa to their aid. From this time a change came over the nature of the struggle, which became one between Cross and Crescent. The Arab element in the Moslem population was swamped after the arrival from Africa first of the Almoravides, and then of the Almohades; while Crusaders from all parts of Europe came to fight in the Christian ranks. The nature of the struggle changed for the worse, and it became dominated by a feeling of bitter animosity between the combatants, in which the chivalry often displayed in earlier days was abandoned.

Powers of the Church

The metamorphosis of a political war into a religious one naturally increased the powers of the Church, which was always inclined to show itself more intolerant in Spain than elsewhere, and it used all its influence to keep alive the crusading spirit. For centuries life to the Spanish was one long Crusade. When the conquest of Granada in 1492 deprived their spirit of its outlet against the Moors in the Peninsula, there were the Turks in the eastern Mediterranean to take their place; after that came the Reformation, and the war against Protestantism. The idea that Spain was the chosen instrument of God for the chastisement of Moslems and heretics grew up so rapidly during the reconquests that it became an obsession, and it was not until the nation was prostrate with exhaustion in the early years of the nineteenth century that the crusading spirit may be said to have been exhausted.

The progress of the Christian armies was by no means uninterrupted after the capture of Toledo, for in the year following that event Alfonso VI was routed by the Almoravid hosts near Badajoz. Nevertheless Islam was slowly pushed back, and in 1094 Valencia was taken by the Cid, that picturesque figure who, having sold his services in turn both to Cross and to Crescent, posthumously became a Spanish national hero. For nearly a hundred years civil

wars then weakened both parties, but there was constant
fighting, and the Moors were losers on the balance. In 1140
the kingdom of Portugal was founded, and seven years later
Lisbon became its capital. The last great counter-offensive
of the Moors took place towards the end of the twelfth
century, when the Almohades defeated Alfonso VIII of
Castille at Alarcos in 1185. This victory, however, had no
permanent consequences, for in 1212 Alfonso VIII, at the
head of a great army of Crusaders, routed the Moors at the
battle of Las Navas de Tolosa, which secured for ever
the preponderance of Christianity in Spain. After this the
work of reconquest proceeded apace. Ferdinand III of
Castille occupied successively Cordova, Seville, and Cadiz,
and within fifty years of their defeat at Las Navas de
Tolosa the Moors were confined within the limits of the
little kingdom of Granada.

Representative Government

After the land had been won back the task of the organization of these new conquests was taken in hand, and on
its constitutional side this was of great importance. It is not
generally realized that the principle of representation was
adopted in Spain earlier than in England, for in Navarre it
can be traced as far back as the fourth decade of the
twelfth century. Medieval Spain regarded the social elements represented in its Cortes (*i.e.* parliament) as parts of
a living entity, with a separate and autonomous individ-
uality, but subordinate to the existence of the whole, and
this was the basis upon which the Cortes of a Spanish kingdom rested at this time. Slightly different conditions
obtained in the various kingdoms. In León borough representatives sat with those of the nobles and clergy after
1116, and in Castille from a somewhat later date. In Aragón
the Cortes was composed of four *Brazos* or Estates, namely
the high nobility, the knights or landed gentry, the clergy,
and the towns and universities, though it is to be noted that
all the nobles had not the right to attend unless specially
summoned by the king. In Catalonia the organization was

on somewhat similar lines, with the exception that there were three *Brazos* instead of four, and in Valencia it was the same as in Catalonia. In all the kingdoms the towns played a very important part.

The withdrawal of the Moslems left large tracts of land available for settlement by the conquerors, and no inconsiderable proportion was somewhat inadvisably awarded to the military orders, thus strengthening still further the position of the Church. These bodies had come into exist-ence during the reconquest, and there were four of them, namely the Orders of Calatrava, Alcántara, Montesa, and Santiago. For many years they formed a considerable obstacle to the Crown, and it was not until the Spanish monarchs hit upon the happy expedient of combining in their own persons the Grand Mastership of the Orders that they ceased to be a thorn in their side. The Mozarabs, that is to say the Christians who had accepted Moslem rule, soon amalgamated with their co-religionists from the north, but there still remained a strong Moorish and Jewish element in the population, particularly in Andalusia and Murcia. Nor was the Moorish influence by any means wholly at an end in intellectual matters, though the greatest brain in Moslem Spain, Averroes, had died in 1198, for Alfonso X of Castile, 'The Wise', was much affected by it. Alfonso was, it must be confessed, very largely a theorist, for his famous *Siete Partidas* laid down doctrines which he was unable to apply. Nevertheless, he made Castillian, rather than Galician or Aragonese, the language of Spain.

A Centrifugal Civilization

The reconquest from the Moors of all but a fraction of the Peninsula did not result in the unification of Christian Spain. The kingdom of Portugal had early established its independence, and although León was finally united with Castile, the other states, namely Aragón and Navarre, remained apart. The history of them all is the record of civil wars and disputed successions, varied by occasional intervals of strong rule. Nevertheless, there was one

important difference, due to geographical reasons, between
the evolution of Castille and that of Aragón, which was
to have a great influence upon the subsequent development
of Spain. Castille looked to the west and to the Atlantic,
while the gaze of Aragón was directed rather to the east and
to the hegemony of the Mediterranean. Sicily and Sardinia
became Aragonese possessions, while in the middle of the
fifteenth century an illegitimate branch of the ruling
dynasty in Aragón ascended the throne of Naples. During
the later Middle Ages, too, Catalan sailors and mercen-
aries played no inconsiderable part in the politics of the
dying eastern Empire and when the Turks captured
Constantinople in 1453 the seriousness of the situation was
at once felt in Aragón. Furthermore, Castille had always
been friendly with France, while the wars of Aragón
against the Angevin monarchs of Naples, and her intrigues
in Navarre, had resulted in the establishment of definitely
bad relations with her northern neighbours. In 1479 the
kingdoms of Aragón and Castille became united in the
persons of Ferdinand V and Isabella I.

The union of the two kingdoms was purely personal,
and was comparable with that of England and Scotland
on the accession of James VI and I to the throne of the
former. The two states did not become one, but remained
distinct units, each with its own laws and institutions.
There was no King of Spain as such, just as there was no
common Cortes, and the monarch ruled his dominions
under a variety of titles. This fact contributed largely to the
weakness of Spain in her long struggle with France, which
was much more centralized. From the days of the Visigoths
the centrifugal forces have rarely been far below the surface
in the Peninsula.

CHAPTER TWO

Spain as a Great Power, 1492-1808

The first task of Ferdinand and Isabella, after the union of the Spanish kingdoms in their own persons, was the conquest of the Moorish realm of Granada, and this was finally accomplished in 1492. There can be no doubt that a strong appeal was made, in order to obtain recruits for the enterprise, to the crusading spirit and to the deep religious feelings which were so strong in the Spain of that day, but the policy which inspired the attack on Granada was dictated by political necessity. The Crescent, as typified by the Ottoman Sultan, was supreme in the eastern Mediterranean, and although there was a lull in Turkish operations after the death of Mohammed II in 1481, the next generation saw the Turks supreme in north Africa, as well as hammering at the gates of Vienna. The kingdom of Granada was the last foothold of Islam in the Peninsula, and the Catholic Sovereigns, as Ferdinand and Isabella were termed, feared that if they delayed the Moors would call the Turks to their aid. This was a very real danger, for in any case, the port of Malaga was in Moslem hands, and the threat was only averted by the conquest of Granada, which finally drove Islam out of Spain.

Expulsion of the Jews

In the same year (1492) there also took place the expulsion of the Jews. In this case, too, an appeal was made to religious prejudice to achieve what was primarily a political purpose.

Rightly or wrongly, the Jews had long been regarded as

extremely partial to the Moorish cause, and it was very largely to combat their activities that the Inquisition had been introduced into Castille in 1470. The Inquisition in Spain was always as much of a secular as of a clerical organization, and it was rather an instrument of policy on the part of the State than of the Church. At the same time, the two were so interwoven that it was impossible to say where the one began and the other finished, and the expulsion of the Jews is a case in point: indeed it would probably have taxed the ingenuity of Isabella herself to say whether she attacked the Jews because she considered them to be the enemies of Christianity or of Spain.

Discovery of America

If the conquest of Granada and the expulsion of the Jews were in no small degree a legacy from the past, the discovery of America in the same year was an investment for the future. The wealth from the New World enabled Spain for upwards of a century to play a predominant part in the politics of Europe that would otherwise have been denied to her, while the work to be done in America was pre-eminently suited to the national genius. The *conquistadores* firmly believed that they had a mission to spread the Christian religion in the lands they discovered, while the small amount of support they received from home gave full scope for that individualism which is the most prominent national characteristic. In spite of the atrocities that too often marked the progress of the Spaniards in America, though these were no worse than those practised by their English and French contemporaries, the work they accomplished there represented a solid gain for civilization as a whole. The old cultures of the New World may seem attractive in retrospect, but they had no very deep roots, and were not far removed from barbarism. Spain took across the Atlantic all that she had inherited from Imperial Rome, and in spite of the innumerable revolutions which have marked the history of Latin America, what she effected there has remained substantially unshaken.

• •

Charles V on horseback, by Titian

2 Philip II, by Pantoja de la Cruz

3 Cervantes, author of Don Quixote

Charles III by Goya

5 *Alfonso XIII and Primo de Rivera*

6 *General Franco and H.R.H. Don Juan Carlos in June 1971, at the military parade celebrating the 32nd anniversary of Franco's victory in the Spanish Civil War*

By the end of the fifteenth century the Cortes, like similar legislative institutions in all parts of Europe, had lost much of its power, though it continued to be stronger in Aragón than in Castille. The Catholic Sovereigns took advantage of this to increase the power of the Crown, and they governed through councils, of which there were eleven in all, just as their Tudor contemporaries were doing in England. The Council of State dealt with questions of foreign policy; the Council of Castille acted as a judicial body, drafted laws, and possessed appellate jurisdiction; the Council of the Indies had charge of the administration of the Americas; and the Council of the Inquisition was concerned with matters of religion. This system of administration had, in theory, much to recommend it, and so long as the monarchs of Spain were served by men of the ability of Cardinals Mendoza and Cisneros it did work quite well, but with the passage of time over-centralization set in, and paralysis was too often the result.

Results of Inflation

The financial system proved no more capable than the political of standing the test of time, and the incidence of taxation was calculated to inflict the maximum amount of damage upon commerce, while producing the minimum revenue. Such being the case, it is not surprising that the boom of the first half of the sixteenth century was followed by a slump. There was a tax upon all sales, while goods in transit from one part of Spain to another were subject to many duties of various sorts. The export of cattle and corn was forbidden, but foreigners were allowed, in return for loans, to compete in the home market in a way detrimental to the native producers. Indeed, it was often cheaper to buy goods from abroad than those from another province.

In normal circumstances this system would have been difficult enough to work, but the circumstances were not normal, for the steady influx of precious metals from the Americas was resulting in galloping inflation. In the middle of the sixteenth century, for example, house rents in

2—ASHOS * *

Valladolid, then the capital of the Spanish Empire, rose within a decade by anything from 50 to 80 per cent. The statesmen of that age were just as bewildered by currency problems as are those of today, and, faced with a rapid rise in prices, they merely applied the old methods with increased vigour. Spain was not a rich country, and with her resources crippled by a myriad economic restrictions she was in the end unable to maintain her position as the leading power in Europe. What is remarkable is not that she lost her supremacy so soon, but that she retained it for so long, for she was the greatest nation in the world at any rate until 1640.

The Italian Scene

What Spain required on the morrow of the conquest of Granada was a period of peace during which the country could adapt itself to the changed circumstances brought about by unification and the discovery of America: what she got was a long series of wars which made it impossible to undertake any reforms at home. In 1494 Charles VIII of France invaded Italy, then divided into a number of small states, and unless Spain wished to see the whole balance of power in the Mediterranean upset to her disadvantage it was clear she would have to fight. Ferdinand was by no means averse to this for interference in Italian affairs had become a tradition in Aragón, and now he had the resources of Castille too upon which to draw. The war continued intermittently until the middle of the following century, by which time Spain had become the dominant power in Italy, thereby in all probability saving that country from becoming a Turkish province. On the whole this situation was an advantage to Spain, for the possession of Italy not only provided her with some excellent soldiers and skilful generals, such as Parma and Spinola, but the control of the Neapolitan and Sicilian ports enabled her to carry on the struggle against the Turks in the eastern Mediterranean instead of off her own coasts.

Spanish Armed Forces

What enabled Spain to bestride the world like a colossus during the whole of the sixteenth and the first half of the seventeenth century was her incomparable infantry, the creation of Gonsalvo de Córdoba. Divided into *tercios* some six thousand strong, it dominated the battlefields of Europe, and it always contained a high proportion of foreigners, including Irish, in its ranks. There was plenty for the *tercios* to do, for Ferdinand and Isabella had no son who succeeded them, and their heir was their elder daughter, all too soon to be known as Juana the Mad : she married a Habsburg Archduke, and that brought Spain into the political complications of central Europe, for in due course their son, Charles, succeeded not only to the dominations of the Catholic Sovereigns but also to the Low Countries and the Franche Comté, the possessions of his father's family, while he was elected, as Charles V, to be Holy Roman Emperor, as well, thus achieving a position never held by any man before or since.

These events had disastrous consequences for Spain. Her true interests lay in the Mediterranean and in the New World, but the circumstances of her monarch distracted her energies to the Netherlands and central Europe. On all sides the possessions of Charles surrounded France, and on repeated occasions she attempted to break out : this, in its turn, compelled Spain to strive to keep her enemy encircled, and so the struggle went on until in 1700 the day came when Louis XIV was able to place his grandson upon the Spanish throne. As if this were not enough, the Reformation took place in the early years of Charles, and it was to Spain that he looked for the resources which might enable him to make headway against those who professed the new religion, while in due course the championship of the Roman Catholic Church meant war with England and the revolt of the Netherlands. Spain could not at one and the same time colonize the Americas, hold the Turks (with whom the French King as often as not allied) at bay, keep France encircled, sustain the Austrian Habsburgs, and dispute the mastery of the seas with England.

A Weakening Economy

Above all there was the steadily worsening economy. It was an age when international credit as we know it today was non-existent, and therefore actual gold was necessary for a war-chest: yet the more the Spaniards distributed their gold throughout Europe the worse the inflation grew, until the deficit in the revenues in Lombardy had to be made good by Naples and Sicily, and sometimes from the Peninsula itself, which was poor enough anyhow, while all the time the blood and treasure of Spain were being wasted in quarrels in which she had nothing to gain and everything to lose.

The Reign of Charles V and I

Charles had been brought up in the Low Countries, and was more of a Fleming than a Spaniard. He could not speak Spanish, and met with a very cold reception when he first visited the Peninsula. The advancement of Flemings to high office also caused bitter hostility towards the new monarch, and in 1520 Castille broke out into open rebellion. The towns were the chief instigators of the rising, for they saw their old privileges disappearing one by one before the increase of the royal power. In the end the revolt was crushed at Villalar in 1521, not least because it was developing into a social war, and those who had anything to lose were forced into the Royalist ranks. Charles, however, had learnt his lesson, and before many years were past he had become as good a Spaniard as any of his subjects. Nevertheless, the story of his life belongs rather to the annals of Germany than to those of Spain.

At the same time it would be unfair to say that Charles was unmindful of Spanish interests; rather was it that he was so busy in Germany that he had not the necessary time to devote to them. The Pyrenees had already become the Spanish frontier to the north with the annexation of southern Navarre in 1512, and Charles was careful to maintain his hold there. He also resisted all attempts on the part of France to regain a foothold in Italy, and in 1525 the French sustained at Pavia one of the greatest defeats in their history, when Francis I was himself taken prisoner by the Spaniards. Nor did Charles neglect what had become the historic mission to defend the western Mediterranean against the Turks and the Barbary Corsairs. In 1535 he led an expedition against Tunis, which he captured, and had he immediately proceeded against the other Moslem strongholds he might have anticipated by over three centuries the work of France in occupying the coast of north Africa; unfortunately, his attention was distracted elsewhere, and when he attacked Algiers in 1541 he met with a severe reverse. Thereafter the Barbary Corsairs continued their raids upon the shores of Spain, and thousands of Spanish men and women were sold in the slave-markets of the Ottoman Empire. Charles had no time to do any one thing properly.

Accession of Philip II

In 1555 he took the first step in relieving himself of the responsibilities that were proving too much for him. 'Fortune is a strumpet,' he declared, 'and reserves her favours for the young,' so he handed the Netherlands to his son Philip, who was already King of the Two Sicilies and Duke of Milan, and, since his marriage with Mary Tudor, King of England. In the following year the crowns of Spain and the Indies were also transferred to Philip, while in 1550 Charles had secured the election of his brother, Ferdinand, as his successor in the Empire. When all this had been done, the greatest monarch in the world betook himself to the seclusion of the monastery of Yuste, in Extremadura, where he died in the same year at the age of fifty-seven.

With the accession of Philip II there came to the Spanish throne the best known of the kings of Spain, but also of

the one concerning whom there has been the greatest
controversy. Down the centuries it has been assumed in
Anglo-Saxon and Protestant countries that he was the
secular arm of the Counter-Reformation; that in both his
domestic and foreign policy he was inspired primarily by
religious motives; and that he was always working hand-
in-hand with the Papacy; whereas in fact nothing could be
further from the truth. That the King himself believed the
interests of Church and State to be identical there can be
no doubt, and he was continually complaining of the
opposition with which he met from the Holy See. A more
balanced view was that of Pope Sixtus V who wrote that
'the King of Spain, as a temporal sovereign, is anxious
above all to safeguard and to increase his dominions. . .
The preservation of the Catholic religion which is the
principal aim of the Pope is only a pretext for his Majesty,
whose principal aim is the security and aggrandizement of
his dominions.'

Church and State

The fact is that the Pope had no effective power in
Spain at all, and a recent writer has gone so far as to
assert that the domination of the Church by the Crown
was probably more complete in Spain than in any other
part of Europe, including Protestant countries with an
Erastian system. Philip did not create this state of affairs,
he inherited it. Its origins lay in the reaction initiated by
Ferdinand and Isabella against the nepotism of the Papacy
in the previous century, and was thus in origin a measure
of reform. The Holy See gave ground very reluctantly
where the appointment of bishops and abbots was concerned, and it was not until 1523 that Charles V induced
his former tutor, by then Pope Adrian VI, to grant him in
perpetuity the right to appoint to bishoprics; after that
there was no looking back, and by the end of the reign
there were few lucrative clerical benefices in Spain which
were not in the hands of the Crown. That Philip was a
devout Catholic cannot be questioned, but as a king, and

a continually impecunious king at that, the opportunity was too tempting to be ignored; applicants for preferment were only too ready to promise to pay him a percentage of the revenues attached to the office they were seeking, so a royal nepotism succeeded the papal.

The same was true of the Inquisition, and Philip was neither the first nor the last ruler in the world's history to believe that his own interests and those of religion were identical. What is repugnant to the modern mind in the work of the Inquisition is that religion was put at the disposal of a bloodthirsty policy, but it cannot be denied that success, however dearly bought, attended the activities of the Holy Office, for heresy was strangled at birth: it was definitely one of those cases where the blood of the martyrs was not the seed of any Church. Comparisons are proverbially odious, but it is worth noting that between 1563 and 1603 at least 3,400 Scots were burnt for witchcraft, while in retrospect there seems to have been little difference between the position of a Protestant in Spain and that of a Catholic in England, for both Philip and Elizabeth deliberately confounded opposition to their religious policy with treason to the respective states of which they were head.

Foreign Commitments

Spain under Philip II had to meet the liabilities which Charles had incurred on her behalf. In particular there was the *Damnosa Hereditas* of the Low Countries, which were a perpetual source of weakness, and should never have been included in the Spanish dominions. Their possession entailed the control of the sea-route through the English Channel, and with the failure of the Armada in 1588 this became highly insecure. There was, it is true, access to them by land from Lombardy through the Franche Comté, but that depended upon the inability of France to break through her bonds. Philip then found himself compelled to interfere in French internal politics in order to keep France weak, and in the latter part of his reign this

actually necessitated the presence of a Spanish garrison in
Paris. The possession of the Netherlands also roused the
hostility of England, always alarmed at the domination of
the Low Countries by a great power, and this meant the
harrying of Spanish America by English adventurers, and
English assistance to the enemies of Spain in all parts of
Europe: to this Philip replied in kind, notably in Ireland.

The earlier years of the reign were marked by a pro-
longation of the struggle against Islam. After the conquest
of Granada the Moriscoes, that is to say the descendants
of the Moors, had been allowd many privileges, such as
permission to wear the national costume, and although
these were curtailed in 1526, the regulations of that year
were not generally enforced. Philip, however, was under
no illusion about the negotiations which were in progress
between the Moriscoes on the one hand and the Turks
and Barbary Corsairs on the other, or the danger to the
Spanish state which they involved, so he applied measures
so harsh that in 1568 the Moriscoes rose in revolt. For
two years Andalusia and Murcia were the scene of a war
in which quarter was neither asked nor given, but at the
end of that time Philip's troops were victorious.

The settlement was hard on the defeated, as was only
to be expected in view of what was at stake. The Moorish
settlements were broken up, and their inhabitants scattered
in La Mancha, Castille, Extremadura, and Galicia; all
Moriscoes were forbidden under penalty of death to
approach within thirty miles of Granada; and all Arabic
books were ordered to be destroyed, while the possession
of one rendered the unfortunate owner liable to punish-
ment in the galleys. Even these measures did not suffice,
for in 1609 Philip III having discovered that the Moriscoes
were intriguing with the French, completed his father's
work by expelling them from the country altogether.
Meanwhile the war against the Crescent elsewhere was
not neglected, for in 1565 the Viceroy of Naples had saved
Malta from the Turks, and six years later Don John of

Austria, an illegitimate son of Charles V, broke for ever the naval power of the Ottoman Sultan at Lepanto.

Domestic Disappointments

The earlier years of Philip's life were far from being happy even domestically for he was only forty-one when his third wife died in 1568, and the blow was a heavy one for he was always a most devoted husband: that year had already been marked by the death of his eldest son, Don Carlos, in very mysterious circumstances. That the young man had inherited the madness of his grandmother, Juana, is almost certain, but his father, doubtless to conceal the fact, hushed the matter up to such an extent as to put the most sinister interpretation upon his end, for which there was no foundation in fact: indeed he acted more than a little stupidly, and raised more suspicions than he allayed, so it is hardly surprising that in hostile circles he was freely accused of the murder of his own son.

Incorporation of Portugal in Spain

Meanwhile, events in Portugal were moving in a way calculated to enable Philip to complete the work of Ferdinand and Isabella by the political unification of the Peninsula. In 1578, the reigning Portuguese monarch, Sebastian, was killed in battle in Morocco, and he was succeeded by his great-uncle, Henry, formerly a cardinal, who himself died two years later. This led to a disputed succession, for the chief claimants to the vacant throne were Antonio, an illegitimate, but subsequently legitimized, nephew of Henry, and Philip II, whose mother had been Henry's sister. Antonio, being on the spot, met with some success at first, but the King of Spain was infinitely more powerful, and a Spanish army under the Duke of Alba was soon in occupation of Lisbon. In absorbing Portugal into his dominions Philip was acting in the best interests of his kingdom, for not only did Spain thus obtain the use of the harbour of Lisbon and the wealth of Brazil, but her enemies could not make Portugal their base of operations against Castille. Philip was careful not to offend Portuguese susceptibilities, and had his successors displayed the same tact the union of the two countries might well have endured.

The Revolt of the Netherlands

As the years went by the preoccupation of Spain proved to be the Netherlands, which became a veritable running sore. Charles, as a native of the Low Countries himself had not been unpopular there, though he had his difficulties from time to time. The population was varied in every respect. In Flanders, Brabant, and Hainault there were great nobles with large estates; Ghent and Bruges were big cities with an old tradition of independence; while in Friesland there was a race of hardy mariners. In addition, Protestantism was making considerable headway; so that there existed all the ingredients of a crisis of the first magnitude even before Philip determined to introduce the Inquisition and to increase the number of bishoprics. The Protestants were determined to resist both these measures, while Protestants and Catholics were equally resolute in the opposition to all attempts to treat the Netherlands as a Spanish province. Unfortunately for Philip his opponents found a leader in William the Silent, Prince of Orange, and the state of the country grew increasingly more disturbed, until in 1567 the Duke of Alba was sent to stamp out all disaffection. The result was to make matters worse, for Alba found himself compelled to impose taxes which had the most disastrous economic consequences. He was in due course recalled, and was succeeded in turn by Requesens, Don John of Austria, and Alexander Farnese, Duke of Parma.

Yet it was essential to have a loyal Netherlands if the encirclement of France was to be maintained, and as England, under Elizabeth I, was no longer in the sphere of Spanish influence it was advisable to subdue her too, so in her search for security Spain was forced to pursue a policy which necessitated a further straining of her resources. There was more than one attempt or projected attempt at the invasion of Britain, but they all came to nothing, while the failure of the Armada left Spain in north-west Europe even weaker than before, for, as we have seen, it made the sea-route to the Netherlands highly insecure. Nevertheless the conditions in which warfare was carried on in the sixteenth and seventeenth centuries made it possible for Spain to conceal her growing weakness in a way that would have been out of question in a later age. Armies were small in size; they lived to a large extent on the country in which they were operating; they retired into winter quarters for several months of each year; and most campaigns were little more than a succession of sieges. All this enabled Spain to maintain the appearances of her ancient power long after it had ceased to be a reality. She was in possession of all the strategic points on the French frontiers, and as she generally remained on the defensive, she was able to fight for years with the minimum of loss. Even in the days of her decline, during the latter part of the reign of Philip IV (1621–65), her armies were able to threaten Paris.

Centralization

The longer Philip II reigned the more thoroughly did power become concentrated in his hands throughout the Spanish Empire: even where the old constitutional forms were preserved the spirit had departed from them, and no action was taken anywhere without reference to the crowned bureaucrat at the Escorial. The only serious opposition to this state of affairs was made by Aragón, which rose in revolt owing to Philip's interference with the course of justice there in connection with his fugitive secretary, Antonio Pérez. This man had fallen foul of his master, and had fled to Aragón, where he appealed to its ancient liberties and the right of sanctuary. In the end Pérez made his escape to England, but the Aragonese rebellion was crushed. The Cortes of that kingdom was deprived of all control over military and financial matters, and its veto was abolished. It may be remarked, however, that centralization in the sixteenth century did not imply what it would today. Means of communication were too primitive, and the machinery of administration was too rudimentary. What Philip did was to concentrate all effective power in the hands of the Crown, but Galicia and Andalusia remained as foreign to one another as ever, and there was no common system of government throughout the whole Peninsula. To the modern mind Spanish administration at the death of Philip II in 1598 would have seemed a synonym for chaos.

The Escorial

Probably the greatest material relic of Philip is the royal monastery of San Lorenzo Del Escorial some thirty miles from Madrid. Its foundation was in consequence of a vow that he had made when his troops won the battle of St Quentin over the French on St Lawrence's Day, namely 10 August 1557: it was to be built in the form of the gridiron on which the saint had been martyred. To use the King's own words the vow was 'to build a palace for God, with just a cell for my humble self, where my tired limbs can dwell until death calls me', and no one can come away from the Escorial without the consciousness of having been in the presence of one of the greatest works of man.

Estimate of Philip II

To sum up the reign of Philip II. So far as domestic affairs are concerned the evidence would seem to show that the economic decline of Spain really began after his death except for the galloping inflation, but that even so it was a great deal slower than is usually stated. As for Spain's position in the world it was surely on balance a great deal stronger when the King died than it had been when he succeeded to the throne. It is true that England had slipped from his grasp, but she was a nuisance rather than a menace; Philip had also lost part of that *Damnosa*

Hereditas, the Low Countries, but he had united the Iberian Peninsula, and completed the work of Ferdinand and Isabella, by the incorporation of Portugal in his dominions, while the Spanish possessions in the New World had been rounded off by the annexation of Brazil. France was no more formidable than she had been fifty years before, and Spanish armies were to play a considerable part in French politics for many years to come; it was also largely his doing that Germany remained half-Catholic, which, rightly or wrongly, was his policy that she should be.

The century which elapsed between the death of Philip II in 1598 and that of Charles II in 1700 falls into two clearly-defined periods. During the reigns of Philip III and Philip IV Spain was in reality growing weaker, but the fact passed unnoticed by the outside world. Accordingly, the rest of Europe, excluding of course the dominions of the Austrian Habsburgs, was still arrayed against her, and even Oliver Cromwell thought the Spain of Philip IV the same menace as that of Philip II. The second period began in 1665, when a series of French victories at last demonstrated the decrepitude of the Spanish Empire. Thereafter Spain was for a time the Sick Man of Europe, and the great problem was the disposal of his inheritance once Charles II, the last of the Spanish Habsburgs, was dead. In the meantime such old enemies as the English and Dutch did all they could to preserve the Spanish dominations against the encroachments of Louis XIV.

The Golden Age of Spanish Literature and Art

In spite, however, of the decline of Spanish power at this time this was the Golden Age of Spanish civilization: both Philip III and Philip IV were patrons of literature and art, in which Spain continued to lead the world. The Spanish theatre was the pattern upon which the European stage still modelled itself, and the great Lope de Vega did not die until 1635, or Tirso de Molina until 1648, while Calderón was at the zenith of his fame in the last years of Philip IV. The reverses suffered by the Spanish armies at the hands of the French, and the growing poverty of the country, were entirely without influence upon its literature and art, so that in the seventeenth century they reached their heyday: during the course of it Cervantes published both *Don Quixote* and the *Novelas Ejemplares*: there flourished the great satirist Quevedo; and in art the period was distinguished by Ribera, Zurbarán, Murillo, and, above all, Velázquez.

CHAPTER THREE

Spain as a Great Power 1492-1808
(continued)

Philip III and Philip IV were far from being fools, but they were too indolent by nature to devote their whole lives to the working of the administrative machine which Philip II had perfected, and so power passed into the hands of their favourites, respectively the Duke of Lerma and the Count Duke of Olivares.

Lerma as Chief Minister

Lerma realized his country's need of repose after her many activities in the preceding reign, and in 1609 he made a truce of twelve years with the Dutch. He also took advantage of the accession of the pacific James I to the throne of England to make peace with him. When Henry IV of France was murdered in 1610, Lerma arranged a double marriage between the royal families of France and Spain, and so put an end to the ambitious designs which the dead monarch had harboured against the Spanish dominions in Italy. All this was very well, and had Lerma also pursued a policy of retrenchment at home he might have arrested the decline of Spain. Instead, there was the wildest extravagance, even allowing for the contemporary inflation and fall in the value of money. Philip III spent 1,300,000 ducats a year on his household, whereas that of his father had cost only 400,000. The Duchy of Milan had an annual deficit of 200,000 ducats, and the Two Sicilies one of double that amount. In addition every office in the state was openly sold by Lerma and his friends:

whatever the regime those who exercise power must always bribe those upon whom that power depends, and Lerma had to buy the support of courtiers who would otherwise have plotted his downfall.

The Thirty Years' War

Even the boon of peace was not enjoyed for long, since in 1618 there began the Thirty Years' War, and into that conflict Spain was inevitably drawn, partly by the necessity of maintaining the encirclement of France, and partly owing to the dynastic relationship with the Austrian Habsburgs. Once more Spanish lives and Spanish money were spent in a cause which was no concern of Spain, while as a master of diplomacy Olivares proved no match for his great rival, Richelieu. During the course of this struggle Spain received two blows, one at sea and the other on land, which were to prove mortal. In 1639 the Spanish fleet was defeated by the Dutch in the Downs, and henceforth the sea-route to the Low Countries was closed in time of war. Four years later the French under Condé broke the incomparable infantry of Spain at Rocroy, and Spanish supremacy in the field, which had lasted since the days of Gonsalvo de Córdoba, came to an end. Only the deaths of Louis XIII and Richelieu, and the outbreak of civil war in France in the shape of the Fronde, saved Spain from complete overthrow at this time.

Portugal Becomes Independent

It was indeed lucky for Philip IV and his subjcts that the French were in no condition to take advantage of their misfortunes, for the Spanish Empire appeared to be on the verge of dissolution. Olivares had brought in a fresh horde of hungry place-seekers, who devoured anything that had been left by Lerma and his friends. In his anxiety to satisfy them the Count Duke bethought himself of Portugal, and, throwing all discretion to the winds, filled the more lucrative Portuguese offices with Spaniards. This precipitated a revolt in 1640, and Portugal regained her independence in spite of every effort by Spain to reconquer her. Separatism is always dormant in the Peninsula, and it was only with some difficulty that in the same year Andalusia was prevented from going the same way as Portugal. More dangerous was the revolt of Catalonia, which transferred its allegiance to the King of France, and for some years French and Spaniards fought there and in Aragón, for Castille never wavered in its loyalty to the Crown. In Italy the situation was no better, for a naval action off the coast of Tuscany in 1646 had given the command of the Mediterranean to France for the first time, and two years later Naples rose in revolt under Masaniello. Everywhere the middle years of the seventeenth century were marked by unrest largely due to rampant inflation.

Peace of the Pyrenees

The French not only allowed the Spaniards to reconquer Catalonia and many of the frontier towns in the Netherlands, but in 1653 a Spanish army actually threatened Paris once again. This proved to be the last exhibition of the military power of Spain, for in 1657 Britain, somewhat inadvisedly from her own interests, joined France against her, and Philip could not continue the struggle. The Peace of the Pyrenees two years later ceded Artois, Roussillon, and Cerdagne to France, but although the latter gained a great increase of territory she was still encircled by the Spanish dominions.

In 1665 Philip IV died, and was succeeded by his son, Charles II, nicknamed 'The Bewitched'. Both physically and mentally the new monarch was under-developed, and the question of the succession was of prime importance during his reign, for he was the last of the Spanish Habsburgs. Hardly was Philip dead than Louis XIV claimed the Low Countries by virtue of his queen, the deceased monarch's daughter by his first wife, and in the campaign which followed Spain proved quite incapable of defending her possessions. Complete disaster was only averted by the Triple Alliance of Great Britain, Sweden, and the United Provinces, but, even so, a whole string of Spanish border fortresses were handed over to France by the Treaty of Aix-le-Chapelle in 1668. This proved to be a mere truce, for before Charles II died there were three more wars in which Spain was involved, though it would not be accurate to say that she took an active part in them, for she had sunk too low to maintain an army of any size in the field. The forces of various nations marched to and fro across Spanish territory, and fought battles there when it suited their purpose, and Spain was unable to stop them. By the Treaty of Nimwegen in 1678 France acquired the Franche Comté, and thus broke the bonds which had fettered her since the days of Charles I. For the Spaniards this meant that the land-route from Lombardy to the Netherlands was closed, and their protection from France henceforth depended upon the English and the Dutch.

Problem of the Succession

Meanwhile, in Madrid there was no realization of what was happening, and Spanish pride was as great as it had been when Spanish arms were invincible. What trade was left was in the hands of foreigners, and the capital swarmed with beggars, but the unrest of the earlier part of the century had passed away, for the value of money was now stable once more, presumably owing to the diminution in the flow of precious metals from the Americas. It was clear that the Dauphin, the eldest son of Louis XIV, was the heir by blood, but his mother had renounced all claim to the Spanish throne when she married. The Electress of Bavaria was next in succession, but her mother had made a similar renunciation. The Emperor Leopold I was the third claimant, and he had the advantage that his mother had not renounced any of her claims. If, therefore, the renunciations were to hold, the Emperor had the best claim, if not, then the rightful heir was the Dauphin.

Rival Parties

The Spaniards were divided into an Austrian and a French party, and this division foreshadowed a state of affairs that has existed intermittently down to the present day. At the end of the seventeenth century, as again during the reign of Alfonso XII, the regency of his widow, and the two world wars of our own time, there has been a difference of opinion whether the best interests of the country would be served by an agreement with the western or one of the Germanic powers. On this occasion it mattered little what the Spaniards thought, for the rest of Europe settled the question for them. There were two abortive Partition Treaties before Charles II died, and left the whole of his dominions to Philip, Duke of Anjou, a son of the Dauphin, in the belief that he alone could preserve them intact. This brought about the War of the Spanish Succession, in which Great Britain, the United Provinces, and the Emperor Leopold I fought to place Leopold's son, the Archduke Charles, on the throne of Spain. In the end they failed, not least because Philip had managed to win the hearts of the Castillians, though the Catalans fought for his rival; but by the Treaty of Utrecht in 1713 the new King of Spain found himself shorn of the Netherlands and of the Italian possessions of his predecessor. It was during the course of this conflict that Great Britain helped herself to Gibraltar.

The End of the Habsburgs

The passing of the Habsburgs, which this settlement involved, meant in many ways the passing of old Spain. Under their rule Spanish civilization had reached its zenith, and had left an ineffaceable impression upon the culture of the world for all time: with the advent of the Bourbons much of this was changed, and for a number of years from the monarch downwards it became the fashion to imitate almost slavishly everything that was French.

Coming of the Bourbons

If the links with traditional Spain were often unnecessarily broken, Philip V (1700–46) and his ministers took great interest in every form of public education, and to the first Bourbon monarch is due the foundation of the various Royal Academies which have played so prominent a part in the cultural life of the country during the last two hundred years. The King's example was widely followed, and it was not unusual to find members of the high aristocracy, such as the Conde de Fernan Nuñez, providing primary schools for both sexes on their estates, for he established 'a house of education for poor orphan girls, in which they should be brought up to be good mothers of families, not being required to take the veil, wear monastic dress, or do anything appertaining to the education of nuns.' Women, it may be added, especially the women of the aristocracy, helped a great deal in this revival of culture; they, too, founded primary schools, and furthered the spread of knowledge in every possible way. Most important of all were the *Sociedades Económicas de Amigos del Pais*, which were founded by private enterprise, but were much encouraged by the State. They united all those who were open to new ideas and were inspired by a desire for the regeneration of Spain, while to their initiative were due the creation of classes for artisans, the holding of literary and scientific discussions, and investigations of an industrial or agricultural character. It may thus be said that if the French influence in literature and the arts under the earlier Bourbons was not infrequently to be deplored, in the sciences and in the general arrangement of life it was certainly not without its uses.

The Revival of Spain

This revival of Spain in the eighteenth century is, like its comparable revival under General Franco, a tribute to its resilience: where its industry and commerce were concerned it was the work of several ministers, of whom Patiño, Alberoni, and Ripperdá were prominent, and it was effected in the first place by a reform of the system of taxation. Means of communication were improved, schemes of internal colonization were put into operation, and Spanish shipping was encouraged by subsidies and bounties. As a natural consequence of this policy efforts were made to develop the American colonies, and this brought Spain into conflict with Great Britain, whose interests in the New World were also now considerable. The whole eighteenth century was one long record of accusations of bad faith by one party or the other, and although there might be nominal peace between the two powers in Europe there was generally unofficial war between their respective nationals in the Americas. This had the effect of bringing Spain and France closer together in opposition to their common British foe, a result which was also being brought about by the close relationship of the French and Spanish monarchs, and by Philip's need of French support in his Italian policy.

The Family Compact

Philip had not always been on such good terms with his French relatives, for in spite of the fact that he was compelled by the Treaty of Utrecht to renounce all claim to the throne of France, he still considered himself to be the heir of Louis XV until the latter had children of his own. This brought him into conflict with two successive French regents, the Dukes of Orleans and Bourbon, and there were actually hostilities. As the hope of becoming King of France receded into the distance Philip changed his policy, and until the outbreak of the French Revolution the two Courts generally acted together, more particularly after the Family Compact between them in 1761. In spite of the opposition of the other powers, Philip was conspicuously successful in his Italian schemes, and one son, Charles, became King of the Two Sicilies, and another, Philip, became Duke of Parma. It would doubtless have been more consonant with the interests of Spain had Philip paid greater attention to the Americas, and less to

Italy, but there was a case to be made out for not allowing the latter to pass completely under the control of Austria, since Spain was so closely affected by any alteration in the balance of power in the Mediterranean; furthermore, there was the centuries' old tradition of Spanish interference in Italian politics. Above all there was the influence of Philip's Italian and second wife, Elizabeth Farnese, who was always prompting him to warlike adventures in her native land.

Progress under Ferdinand VI

Philip V was succeeded by his son by his first marriage, Ferdinand VI (1746–59), who was married to Barbara of Braganza, daughter of John V of Portugal. The wits of Madrid said that Queen Barbara had succeeded Queen Elizabeth, and there was something in the jest, but the effect upon the destinies of Spain were very different. Ferdinand was by nature of the most pacific disposition, and his favourite motto was '*Paz con todos y guerra con nadie*' (Peace with all and war with none). When he died he was buried in the Monasterio de las Salesas Reales in Madrid, for like his father he refused to be interred in the Escorial. There were engrossed on his tomb the words, 'Here lies King Ferdinand VI, the best of princes; he died childless, but with a numerous issue of patriotic virtues.' It is true that, like his father, he was much under the influence of his wife, but whereas Elizabeth had encouraged Philip in an aggressive foreign policy in order to place her sons upon Italian thrones, Barbara shared to the full her husband's peaceful intentions. She had no children for whom to provide, and the Portuguese are not a bellicose people, so that her influence was always exercised on the side of peace; with the result that Ferdinand's reign was one of the most tranquil in Spanish history, and both King and Queen devoted their energy to promoting the best interests of their country.

Ferdinand was fortunate in his ministers, especially Ensenada and an Irishman of the name of Wall. They and the King fully realized that it would be madness to think in terms of an army equal to that of France and a navy of the same size as the British; what they aimed at was the raising of the military and naval strength of Spain to a position which would enable her to make her neutrality effective, and to maintain her independence in the councils of the world: this they may be said to have achieved. The financial and economic policy of Patiño was continued: further attention was paid to agriculture, roads were improved, canals made, and manufacturers assisted in every possible way. The Spanish mines were re-opened, and the ban on the export of metal was removed, while a royalty of 3½ per cent in Spain and 6 per cent in the Americas was imposed. The farming of taxes was abolished, and the revenue rose by five million ducats a year. When Ferdinand VI died Spain was once more a prosperous nation, with a powerful fleet, and three millions sterling in the treasury.

Charles III. The Greatest of the Bourbons

Being childless, Ferdinand VI was succeeded by his half-brother, Charles III (1759–88) who was already King of the Two Sicilies, but he immediately relinquished his Italian possessions to a son, Ferdinand, as it was clear that the powers would not tolerate the re-incorporation of the Neapolitan kingdom in the Spanish dominions. Charles III was an excellent example of those 'enlightened despots' who were so prominent a feature of the latter half of the eighteenth century. He was easily the best and the most intelligent of the Bourbon kings of Spain. With something of the yokel about his appearance, and with a long, pointed nose and piercing blue eyes, he had a strange mask of a face which recalled Louis XI of France. There was, too, something of the *dilettante* about him; he was a lover and patron of the arts; and he was essentially a man of taste upon whom his long residence in Italy, amid the monuments of an ancient civilization, had made a profound impression. Charles was greatly under the influence of French ideas, and this fact goes far to explain his Francophil policy. His motto might well have been, 'Everything for, but nothing by, the people.'

The War of American Independence

During his reign Spain became involved in two major international wars, namely the Seven Years' War, which was at its height when he came to the throne, and the War of American Independence. One of his first acts after his accession was, in 1761, to make another Family Compact with France, which necessitated hostilities with Great Britain, but instead of the support given by Spain to the French cause doing anything to restore the balance in favour of France, it merely involved her in the series of misfortunes which her ally was experiencing, and by the Treaty of Paris in 1763 she was compelled to cede Florida and several West Indian islands to Great Britain. Charles bided his time, and had his revenge when the British American colonies rose in revolt; in 1779 Spain came in on their side, and by the Treaty of Versailles four years later Minorca and Florida became Spanish possessions, though Gibraltar remained British after a notable siege. This treaty marked the zenith of Spanish power in the New World, for in addition to the possession of all central and south America, except Brazil and Guiana, she was mistress in north America of Mexico, California, Louisiana, and Florida.

Charles made no change in his brother's ministers, beyond the addition of the Marquis of Squillacci (Esquilache as the Spaniards called him) to their number, but after the conclusion of the Treaty of Paris, Wall resigned on account of bad sight. He was replaced by Grimaldi, and the two Italians proceeded to accelerate the pace of reform. They made no secret of their determination to limit very drastically indeed the power both of the Church and of the Inquisition, but in doing so they united against themselves elements capable of precipitating a revolt which came within an ace of being a revolution.

Opposition to Reform

The immediate cause of the outbreak was a trifle. For many years the Spaniards had worn wide-brimmed hats, side-locks, and long cloaks (in which daggers were too often and too easily concealed), and they disliked the cocked hats, bag-wigs, and coats in which Charles wished them to appear. In March 1766, an order was issued forbidding the wearing of cloaks beyond a certain length and of wide-brimmed hats, and officials were posted in the streets to cut offending garments to the required dimensions. The attempt to enforce this pragmatism led to rioting and to a demand for the head of Squillacci, who was forced to flee. During the disturbance the Walloon Guards fired on the crowd, and this roused the latter to fury. The Walloon guardsmen were killed at sight, and the capital passed into the hands of the mob: the King was forced to give way, but immediately he had done so he left Madrid for Aranjuez.

Expulsion of the Jesuits

Charles took care that Squillacci got safely out of the country, and then he reformed the administration, placing at its head the Count of Aranda. The new minister was a man of great ability, but also of considerable vanity, and, like his predecessor, he was anti-clerical. During the summer of 1766 the agitation continued, and a plot to murder the King was alleged to have been discovered. Finally, however, Charles got his way, and in December he re-entered Madrid to find his subjects, if still discontented, attired after the new fashion. Both he and Aranda were convinced that the clergy in general, and the Jesuits in particular, had been at the bottom of the trouble, and they were determined to put an end to clerical opposition to their reforms. In their resolution they were greatly influenced by contemporary events in Portugal, where an attempt to murder King Joseph had been laid at the door of the Jesuits, and where the Marquis of Pombal had already adopted strong measures against them.

In April 1767, an order was suddenly issued for the expulsion of the Jesuits from Spain, and it was executed in a manner which inflicted the greatest hardship on those concerned. The priests were not allowed to take anything with them but their personal belongings, and they were conveyed in unseemly haste to the coast, whence they were shipped to such foreign countries as were willing to receive them. The same procedure was adopted in the Americas, with the result that the work of civilization which the Jesuits had been doing in Paraguay came to an end, and the Indians in that country relapsed into savagery. The campaign against the Jesuits was only part of a general offensive against the Church, for Aranda and his master were completely under the sway of the French Encyclopaedists. The Inquisition also became the object of attack, and in 1780 its last victim, an old witch, was burnt alive at Seville – six years, incidentally, before Phoebe Harris met the same fate in front of Newgate. Education, too, which had been taken out of the hands of the Jesuits, was nationalized and secularized.

Effect on the Monarchy

Whether these measures were wise from the point of view of the monarchy is another matter. For centuries the Spanish throne had been invested with a religious sanction, and Church and State had been almost indistinguishable. Charles undoubtedly increased the power of the Crown, but he placed the monarch in a position of dangerous, if splendid, isolation. The Cortes was nothing but a name, the Inquisition was powerless, and the very foundations of the Church were undermined. When the storm came, the monarchy had no outside support upon which it could rely.

The policy of Aranda, and of his successor, the Count of Florida-Blanca, in civil matters was much less open to criticism, and it was largely an intensification of that of Ensenada. In particular, rural depopulation was arrested by internal colonization, and Bavarian immigrants to the number of six thousand were settled in thirteen new villages in the Sierra Morena. The import and export of grain was permitted under certain restrictions with regard to price levels in the home market. A government registry for titles and mortgages was created to render the transfer of land both easy and cheap, and the coinage was reformed and unified. Raw material was allowed to enter the country free, but a prohibitive tariff was put upon such manufactured articles as were likely to compete with Spanish products. The social services also received attention: hospitals, asylums, and almshouses were established all over Spain, as well as savings banks, benefit societies, and philanthropic institutions of one sort and another. The glass factory of La Granja, the porcelain of Buen Retiro, the cotton velvets of Avila, the fine leather of Seville and Cordova, and the fancy goods of Madrid, all became famous at this time, while during the reign of Charles III the population rose by a million and a half to ten million and a quarter.

Growth of Centralization

In many ways from the point of view of internal policy the reigns of Philip V, Ferdinand VI, and Charles III may be regarded as a whole, the Spanish monarchy at this period approaching very closely to the French type with centralization tending to become more complete through the restriction of local privileges. As has been shown, regular ministers replaced the favourites of the previous century, and the *juntas* or councils of government, disappeared, giving place to regular departmental ministries. The nobility and the clergy found themselves more and more subjected to the central authority, and so far as the Church was concerned a Concordat with the Holy See was made in 1754, by which ecclesiastical nominations depended almost entirely upon the King.

Literature and Art

In the intellectual, literary, and artistic spheres there
was, in spite of the efforts of successive monarchs,
certainly a decline in comparison with the great preceding
age, namely that 'Golden Century' which in reality
embraced a period of nearly two hundred years. Literature
was less original, though in certain aspects of it, particularly
in the drama, there was still a very widespread activity.
On the other hand, history more than maintained its
position, for the study of antiquity and the examination of
archives gave birth to such learned publications as
España Sagrada, which was begun by Father Enrique
Flores. Mention has already been made of the foundation
of learned societies: the Royal Spanish Academy was
founded in 1713, the Academy of History in 1738, and
the Academy of Fine Arts of St Ferdinand in 1744.
Charles III, in particular, was distinguished by his taste for
architecture and for painting, and the patronage which he
accorded to the arts and to artists was very considerable
indeed.

At the same time there was no longer the exuberance
or genius of the great period, but architecture in its new
form maintained itself on a level that was still sufficiently
high. There has been much criticism of the style which was
popular at this period with its ornamentation, its luxuriance,
and its overloading, and it has been called 'the romanticism
of rococo'. Yet we owe to it some charming creations, for
example, the Palacio del Marqués de dos Aguas at
Valencia. The same observation applies to baroque in its
classical and grandiose form: Italian, and above all
French influences are certainly recognizable in it, but the
native genius is still preponderant. The Royal Palaces in
Madrid and at Aranjuez, as well as the Castle of San
Ildefonso at La Granja, are very fine specimens of
architecture, and can bear comparison with the very best
work that was being done at that time in other European
countries.

Age of Goya

Painting also held its own. If it had produced nothing more than such an artist like Goya, it could still, thanks to him, be said to have maintained its own prestige. Spanish realism finds its expression in the work of this harsh Aragonese, with a strength and intensity, as well as a psychological penetration hitherto unknown. The new spirit reveals itself in his creations, and in the whole range of his philosophical symbolism. Nevertheless, it is no longer the national realism, the realism of Velázquez, with its depth, and its classical qualities of proportion and complete impersonality. It is a deviation from it, often impetuous and verging on frenzy, towards the fantastic, the grotesque, and the macabre: in short, it is no longer purely Spanish.

What is to be observed in the art of Goya is the keynote of the reign of the earlier Bourbons, for the same deviation from the old realism began to affect the national spirit. Under outside influences, especially those of France, the Spanish soul lost its moral and intellectual unity which in the domain of art as in that of thought, had produced unique works. Foreign ideas began to have their effect upon the national genius, and they were to serve as the ferment of approaching revolutions which were to distract Spain throughout the whole of the nineteenth century.

Charles IV, Maria Luisa and Godoy

The son and successor of Charles III was Charles IV (1788–1808), a worthy man full of good intentions, somewhat like Louis XVI. He was, unhappily, timid, and his character was weak, while he was completely under the domination of his wife, Maria Luisa of Parma: she, in her turn, was wholly influenced by her lover, Manuel Godoy, the guardsman whom she caused to be created successively Duke of Alcudia and Prince of the Peace. The new reign was overshadowed by the outbreak of the French Revolution, and the progress of events in Paris soon brought about a reaction against the reforming policy of Charles III, and at first Spain joined the coalition against France. In 1795, however, Godoy persuaded his master to conclude the Treaty of Basle with the French, and it was for this that he was created Prince of the Peace. Thereafter Spain became the consistent ally of France, and as a result lost not only the islands of Trinidad and Minorca, but also two gallant fleets in the battles of Cape St Vincent and Trafalgar.

Napoleon Appears on the Scene

In spite of this loyalty, Napoleon determined to dethrone the Spanish Bourbons in favour of his brother Joseph, nicknamed 'Pepe Botellas' from his alleged partiality for the bottle, and court intrigues gave him the opportunity which he desired. The heir to the throne, Ferdinand, Prince of the Asturias, was on the worst of terms with his mother's lover, Godoy, and was put in prison for participating in a plot against him. He then appealed to the French Emperor, and Charles IV thereupon followed his example. This caused a riot in Madrid, and with a French army approaching the capital the King did the same thing as his son. Having got both parties exactly where he wanted them Napoleon proceeded to summon them to Bayonne, where, by a mixture of bribery and threats, he induced father and son to abandon their rights to the Spanish throne. The crown was thereupon conferred upon Joseph Bonaparte, who, on 6 June 1808, was proclaimed King of Spain and the Indies.

CHAPTER FOUR

The Last of Old Spain

Napoleon soon discovered that it was one thing to make his brother King of Spain and quite another to render his power in the Peninsula effective. As soon as his intentions became obvious there was a rising in Madrid, and on 2 May 1808, there took place that sanguinary struggle in the Puerta del Sol which has been immortalized by the brush of Goya. In the field, however, the Spaniards were no match for the victors of Austerlitz, more particularly as the armed forces had been 'run down' by Godoy, and a victory of Marshal Bessières at Medina del Rio Seco at the beginning of June enabled Joseph to enter the capital before the end of that month. Punitive columns were then sent out in various directions to secure submission to the new monarch, and it was the disaster which overtook one of these that marked the first step in the downfall of Napoleon.

A French Reverse

At Bailén, in Andalusia, General Dupont, was compelled to lay down his arms with 20,000 men. The news of this surrender, even in those days of imperfect communications, was not long in reaching all parts of Europe, and it encouraged every enemy of Napoleon and of France. In reality the victory had been achieved by the regular Spanish infantry, which, given the opportunity to display them, had not lost its old hard-fighting qualities; but it was generally believed to have been won by armed peasants, and the news that the French veterans had been defeated by such means roused greater enthusiasm.

The Guerrilleros

All over Spain men sprang to arms, and in every district a *junta* was formed to organize resistance to the invaders along the lines which were to be adopted in so many countries during the Second World War, and the struggle which now began was of a nature to appeal to Spanish individualism. Except at Bailén, no regular Spanish force gained a victory over the French, but the *guerrilleros* waged so unceasing a warfare that before long it was highly dangerous for the French troops to move in bodies less than several hundred strong. Their leaders came from all classes of the community, and many of them adopted assumed names to protect their relatives from reprisals on the part of the enemy. It is too often assumed that the French were finally driven out of the Peninsula by Wellington and the British, but although they undoubtedly hastened the end, the chief factor was the Spaniard himself. Whether he was on the offensive or the defensive the *guerrilleros* were Wellington's eyes and ears, and few generals in the course of history have had such advantages in the matter of military intelligence. Wellington used to claim that he could always tell what was happening 'on the other side of the hill', and the claim was just: but that it was just was due to the Spanish people.

The Peninsular War

In spite of the fact that the Spaniards and their British allies emerged victorious from the Peninsular War, or the War of Independence as it is locally termed, it would be difficult to exaggerate the material and moral damage which the struggle inflicted upon the country, and of which the effects were felt for the rest of the nineteenth century: many of Spain's most valuable art treasures were plundered by the French, and even the Escorial lost four organs out of its original eight. All this had the most important

7 *Interior of the mosque at Cordova*

8 (*Overleaf*) *The Roman aqueduct at Segovia*

9 *The Battle of Lepanto, artist unknown*

10 *The Walls of Avila*
11 *The Escorial*

repercussions in the political sphere because the nature of the struggle gave a tremendous fillip to the old centrifugal tendencies, and so undid most of what had been effected by Philip V and his successors. Of all the tragic blunders committed in 1808 the most fatal in its ultimate consequences was the mistake made by Ferdinand VII (1808–33) in placing himself in the power of Napoleon, instead of withdrawing into Andalusia, and putting himself at the head of his people.

Napoleon and the Spaniards

At the same time, the desperate nature of the struggle which began in 1808 cannot obscure the fact that the country was not unanimously in arms on behalf of the absent Ferdinand. It is true that there were few who desired the restoration of his father, but among the educated classes Napoleon did not fail to make some converts to the idea of substituting for the Bourbons a Bonaparte dynasty in the person of Joseph. The French Emperor endeavoured to cover his acts with a cloak of legality by convening at Bayonne a meeting of Spanish magnates, and he presented the gathering with a constitution on the French model. It was quite useless. The Spanish people as a whole would have none of either Joseph or his constitution, and those who were prepared to acquiesce in the change of dynasty were held up to the execration of their fellow-countrymen as *Afrancesados*, while the magnates who had refused the invitation to Bayonne at once became objects of popular adoration.

Joseph, after the defeat of his forces at Bailén, had left Madrid and taken up a position behind the Ebro, where he was in due course joined by the French Emperor in person. Napoleon brought with him the pick of the French army, and he lost no time in falling upon the Spanish armies which had been collected to dispute his advance. Marshal Lannes routed one Spanish force at Tudela, Marshal Soult a second at Burgos, and Marshal Victor a third at Espinosa.

3—ASHOS * *

By the middle of December Napoleon was in Madrid, and the ease with which he had forced his way there gave him a false impression of the nature of Spanish warfare. The result was that in later years he neglected to keep his forces in the Peninsula up to the necessary strength, and he attributed the French defeats to the incompetence of his generals rather than to the obstinate tenacity of their opponents. Meanwhile, the Spaniards had appealed to Great Britain for help, and Sir John Moore was appointed to command the army which had already secured the evacuation of Portugal by the French. For various reasons, of which the difficulty of securing the necessary transport was not the least important, Moore was unable to carry out his instructions to co-operate with the Spaniards, and he finally had to retreat to Corunna, where he was killed in the hour of victory.

Spanish Disaster

The following year, 1809, was one of disaster for Spain. Wellington, to give him the title by which he was soon to be known, succeeded Moore in command of the British forces; he preserved Portugal, and actually defeated the French on Spanish soil at Talavera, but that was all he could effect. Every time that the Spaniards faced their enemies in the field they were routed, and although towns like Zaragoza put up a magnificent defence for a space, by the end of November Cadiz was the only place of importance that was not in French hands. The next two years witnessed little change in Spain itself, and Wellington had his hands full with the preservation of Lisbon from Masséna. In the east the Spaniards again collected an army, but were defeated by Suchet at Albufera. Nevertheless, the resistance to the invaders did not slacken for a moment, and the *guerrilleros* harassed the French at every turn, wearing down their strength month by month. It was a method of warfare with which they did not meet in any other part of Europe.

The Turn of the Tide

In 1812 the tide began to turn, for Napoleon was now at war with Russia and could no longer spare the men necessary to support his brother's unstable throne. Wellington advanced from Portugal, captured the fortresses of Badajoz and Cuidad Rodrigo, and defeated Marshal Marmont at Salamanca in July. The threat which this caused to the line of communication with France caused Joseph to evacuate Madrid, and he fell back behind the Ebro, after withdrawing his troops from Andalusia. Wellington occupied the capital, but was unable to retain it, because a diversion from Sicily, then in British possession, failed at Tarragona and Alicante, while he himself was unable to reduce Burgos. The British had to retreat into Portugal, and Joseph returned to Madrid for what was to prove the last time.

By the spring of 1813 it was clear from the course of events in central Europe that the French Empire was itself tottering, and Wellington determined to take advantage of the fact. He struck once more at the line of communication with France, turned the French position on the Ebro, and in June completely defeated Joseph and Marshal Jourdan at Vittoria. This victory drove the French out of Spain, for it compelled Suchet to abandon his conquests in Valencia, and by the beginning of December the British were investing Bayonne. The attempt to foist Joseph Bonaparte upon the Spanish people had failed. On 22 March 1814, Ferdinand VII re-entered his kingdom by way of Catalonia, but it was to find that much had been changed since he left it six years before.

The Juntas

The events of 1808 had been far-reaching in their consequences both at home and in the Americas. The whole government administration had for so long been centred in the monarch that when he was removed no one knew who was to exercise authority in his place. The Council of Castille made a hesitating attempt to secure the reins of power, but it was too uncertain of its position, and some of its members were too strongly suspected of sympathy with the invaders for the effort to be successful. Meanwhile the *juntas* were springing up all over Spain, and they owed a more or less nominal allegiance to a *Junta Central*, which changed its place of meeting in accordance with the vicissitudes of the military situation. This body was intensely loyal to the absent Ferdinand, and all business was transacted in his name. In 1810 the *Junta Central* repaired to Cadiz, which at that time was one of the few towns not in the hands of the French, and resigned its power to a Council of Regency; before it did this, however, it convoked a Cortes of all Spain in two houses, later reduced to a single chamber. This was a purely revolutionary measure, since no such body was known to the constitution, for the union of the crowns of Castille and Aragón had not been followed by the formation of a united Cortes, as had been the case when León and Castille were united. In effect, it was to prove that a definite break with the past had been precipitated, and an unfortunate precedent had been created, for too often in the years to come one constitutional makeshift after another was to be introduced, either from France or Great Britain, which proved in no way to suit the national genius.

The Constitution of 1812

When the assembly met it at once became evident that two parties were struggling for mastery. On the one side were those who realized how little Spain desired representative government, and how angry Ferdinand would be at such a step having been taken in his absence; on the other side were the men who had become infected with the ideas to which the French Revolution had given birth, and who were determined to take advantage of the suspension of all regular government to put them into practice. The strength of this radical faction lay in the seaports, at that date almost the only part of Spain able to send representatives to the Cortes, and so it is not surprising that the extremists had a majority on that body. The Council of Regency soon found itself unable to work with them, and resigned, only, however, to be succeeded by another more in harmony with the views of the larger part of the deputies. At length, in 1812, the Cortes finished the work upon which it had been engaged (to the almost complete neglect of the conduct of the war against Napoleon, which had been left to Wellington and the *guerrilleros*), and promulgated the constitution which was to take its name from the year that saw its birth.

The main points of this document were that Spain was to be governed by a limited hereditary monarchy, with the right of making laws vested in the Crown and a single chamber. For the election to this chamber all males over the age of twenty-five were to possess the franchise; the actual selection of the deputies was indirect, and involved four separate processes. Whether this scheme could have worked in a country which had been accustomed to representative government for several centuries is doubtful, but that it was totally unsuited to Spain at the beginning of the nineteenth century is certain, for it placed both the Crown and the Church in a subordinate position, and this in spite of the fact they were the only two institutions the country had known since the days of Charles I. All the same it proved attractive all over southern Europe, though it is said that when its enactment was demanded by the Neapolitan insurgents in 1820 there was not a copy to be found in the Kingdom of the Two Sicilies.

Internal Differences

It soon became apparent that the opponents of this measure had gauged the feelings of their fellow-countrymen more accurately than those who supported it, for as the provinces were liberated from the French, and their deputies began to attend the Cortes, the Liberal majority rapidly sunk; this, in its turn, had the effect of rendering the members of that majority the more violent when they realized that power was passing from them. Such was the

situation when the Cortes was dissolved, and a new one
was elected. The most desperate efforts of the Liberals
had only secured them a very narrow majority in the new
house, and they were at once faced with the prospect of
Ferdinand's immediate return from exile. In vain they
attempted to regulate his movements, and to compel him
to take an oath to observe the Constitution of 1812.
Ferdinand temporized until he had ascertained for himself
the state of public opinion, but his journey through
Catalonia was so triumphal a progress that he realized
there was no need for further procrastination; accordingly,
when he arrived at Valencia he condemned the constitution, and restored the old order in its entirety; this step was
accompanied by the arrest of all the leading Liberals.

This early constitutional struggle brought into being the
two parties which were to divide the government between
them for the next hundred years. The Right comprised
the clergy, a large section of the aristocracy, and the overwhelming majority of the nation; while the Left depended
for support upon the middle class and the populace in the
large towns. Nevertheless, the line of demarcation was not
social, and during the whole of the nineteenth century
some of the oldest names in Spain were to be found among
the members of the parties of the Left.

Restoration of Ferdinand VII

The basic weakness of Ferdinand lay in the fact that
having restored the old order he proved quite unable to
make it work. He was far from being the monster of
iniquity that Liberal historians have depicted – after all it
was he who opened the Prado gallery to the public – and
altogether he was by no means an intolerable ruler. The
real charge against his regime was not its tyranny but its
incompetence. Statesmanship of a high order is always
required to steer a country through the difficulties of an
immediate post-war period, and it was notoriously lacking
in Spain at this date. What the outside world thought of
Ferdinand was demonstrated when the troops which his

government raised during the Hundred Days' War were contemptuously refused by the allies, and when Spain at the Congress of Vienna was denied the status of a first-class power for the first time in her history.

Revolt of Spanish America

It was not as if Ferdinand could point to triumphs abroad to counter-balance his mistakes at home, for it was during these years that Spain lost her American colonies. Comparison with the course of events earlier in British North America are meaningless, for the British colonists rejected the yoke of a country which a few years earlier had emerged victorious from the Seven Years' War, while the first blows for South American independence were struck when Spain had been sunk to the lowest pitch of political degradation by Napoleon. Paradoxically enough the revolutionaries originally justified their revolt on the ground that Ferdinand had been set aside for the demo-cratic fashions of a French intruder. Nor was there any resentment at the way in which the colonies were administered from the Peninsula, for, to quote H. A. L. Fisher, 'The colonists experienced no galling sense of vexation from an interfering despotism which was softened by distance, diluted by corruption, and evaded from sloth.'

There was a great deal more to be said for Spanish rule in the New World than is always admitted, for the Spaniards preserved peace over the whole of their vast dominions, and a population, part Spanish, part Creole, part Indian, and part Negro was held together under a common system of policy and belief, to which, however, it must be admitted that Charles III struck a severe blow by the expulsion of the Jesuits, and this loss was not re-paired. Latin America has been more disturbed and less content since Spanish rule came to an end, and the revolt of the Spanish colonies has been to substitute for the long *Pax Hispanica* an era of inter-state rivalries and domestic revolution which is still with us.

Once the revolt had begun it gradually gained ground,

though with a number of setbacks, and in due course only a few years had passed before the island of Chiloe, off the Chilean coast, and the castle of San Juan de Ulloa, which dominates the great Mexican port of Vera Cruz, were practically the only places in the Americas, apart from Cuba and Puerto Rico, that still held out for Ferdinand. In 1824 the final battles were fought which put an end to Spanish rule. In August, Bolivar gained a decisive victory at Junin, and, in December, General Sucre at Ayacucho completely overthrew the Spanish forces, capturing the Viceroy of Peru himself, and all the principal civil and military officials. Many years, however, elapsed before Spain officially recognized the independence of her late colonies; but what is remarkable is that in view of her own internal weakness as a result of the French invasion, Spain should have been able to maintain the struggle in the Americas for so long, and she would not have been able to do so had it not been for the strength of the royalist party among the colonists. In short, the contest which resulted in the independence of the Spanish colonies was largely a civil war, and the support which the King of Spain was able to afford to those who were fighting his battles was at all times negligible from a military standpoint.

Riego's Revolt

While these events were taking place in the New World there had been serious trouble in Spain itself. In 1820 Ferdinand had determined to make one last effort to re-assert his authority in the Americas, and he had accordingly collected all the available forces at Cadiz. Unfortunately, his administration had exercised so demoralizing an effect upon the Spanish marine that there were no transports available, and the troops were kept in idleness pending the arrival of some ships sent by the Tsar. During this period of enforced inactivity the soldiers were an easy prey for the agitators, and in due course one Riego raised the standard of revolt. At first the attempt met with no success, but soon the towns rallied to it, and Ferdinand was forced to give way and promise to abide by the Constitution of 1812. The revolutionaries might, indeed, have been better informed as to the state of the country they were taking over, for when they stormed the prison of the Inquisition in order to set free as they hopefully imagined the martyrs for civil and religious liberty who were languishing there all they found were some ham, some barrels of wine, and a mad French priest, who was comfortably lodged in an attic which he was most unwilling to leave.

They were not long, however, in making a more serious miscalculation, and that was an attack on the Church. To the political demands of the Liberals the majority of the nation was completely indifferent, but when the Church was called into question every peasant felt that a vital principle was at stake. The supporters of throne and altar formed the *Junta Apostólica*, and commenced to harass the new masters of Spain at all points. Nor was this all, for the restored Bourbons in France soon began to feel too close to the Spanish conflagration to be comfortable, and in April 1823, Louis XVIII sent an army of 100,000 men to restore Ferdinand to his former authority which they did without any great difficulty.

Last Years of Ferdinand VII

Thereafter, the last ten years of Ferdinand's reign were a decided improvement upon the earlier period. It is true that the Americas, with the exception of Cuba and Puerto Rico, were lost, but that was inevitable from the moment that Riego raised the standard of revolt. On the other hand, Ballesteros, as Minister of Finance, did much to repair the economic state of Spain: he balanced the budget, drew up a code of commercial law; and promoted the first exhibition of Spanish industries. In this way the position of Ferdinand grew stronger, and evidence of this can be seen with which he held his own after the withdrawal of the supporting French troops in 1828. His rule was not ideal, but it was better than the chaos which had marked that of his opponents.

Abolition of the Salic Law

The real tragedy of the reign of Ferdinand VII was the alteration in the order of succession to the throne, and from this have resulted many of the evils which have afflicted Spain ever since his death. Ferdinand was childless in spite of the fact that he had been married three times, and his heir was his brother, Don Carlos. In 1830, however, he entered into matrimony once more, on this occasion with Maria Cristina of Naples, and in due course it was announced that she was pregnant. This event at once raised a constitutional problem of the first importance, and to appreciate the political and personal passions which have since played so prominent a part in Spanish public life it must be remembered that the principle of the succession had not been settled; indeed, it was very much open to question. The *Siete Partidas* of Alfonso X (1252–84) had recognized the right of females to succeed to the thrones of Castille and León in default of male heirs of an equally near degree of consanguinity, and that this right had also been admitted in practice is proved by the succession of Isabella I (1474–1504); it was recognized, too, in Aragón, for the claim of Charles I was through his mother, Juana the Mad. With the advent of the Bourbons a change was made, and in 1713 Philip V introduced the Salic Law, which established the French procedure of men only.

The matter was still further complicated by the fact that, for some obscure reason, Charles IV, in 1789, convoked the Cortes in secret session, and on his initiative a resolution was passed asking him to revert to the old order of succession, but the necessary decree was never promulgated. In March 1830, Ferdinand VII promulgated the Pragmatic Sanction of his father, and in June of the same year he made a will in which he left the crown to his unborn child. Don Carlos could not, and did not, object to the principle of leaving the crown by will, for it was owing to an act of this nature on the part of Charles II that the Bourbons were in the Peninsula at all, but he protested against the promulgation of the Pragmatic Sanction. He denied that it was genuine, and declared that in any case, since he was alive at the date of its enactment it could not be retrospective. Ferdinand at one time gave way, and revoked the Sanction, but he eventually destroyed the revocation, and when a daughter, Isabella, was born he recognized her as his heir. In 1833 the King died, and then, in his own words, the cork was removed from the fermenting and surcharged bottle that was Spain.

The Carlists

The long reign of Isabella II (1833–68) though nominally constitutional, was in reality a series of military dictator-ships varied by Carlist plots and risings. The supporters of Don Carlos took up arms immediately Ferdinand was dead, and the First Carlist War lasted until 1840. The Carlists, who attracted to their colours both the best and the worst elements in the population, were strong in the Basque Provinces, in Navarre, and in the more mountain-ous districts of Aragón and Catalonia: they also possessed two admirable generals in Zumalacárregui and Cabrera. Their weakness lay in the fact that they were operating from several different quarters, and in their inability to capture the towns, which mostly declared for their opponents. Nevertheless, the termination of the war was in no way decisive, and Carlism with all that it implied remained a very important factor in the national life.

Ferdinand had left his widow, Cristina, as Regent, and at first she and the Prime Minister, Zea Bermudez, showed little inclination to change the method of government; however, they soon discovered that without the support of the Liberals they would be unable to make headway against Don Carlos, and they were therefore compelled to move to the Left. At this time, too, serious disaffection became noticeable among the troops where the apostles of revolu-tionary change were the sergeants, and owing to the incompetence of the officers, due to the absence in the Carlist forces of those who should have held commissions, their influence was even greater than is usually the case. Military risings, *pronunciamientos* as they were called, succeeded one another, and in a mutiny at La Granja the Queen and the Regent were both captured: they were forced to assent to the re-establishment of the Constitution of 1812, after which matters went from bad to worse until a military revolt, headed by Marshal Espartero, overthrew the government, and the Marshal was appointed Regent in place of Cristina.

The Three Marshals

This event ushered in a period during which the three Marshals, namely Espartero, Narvaez, and O'Donnell struggled for power. In their efforts to secure control of their country's destinies they showed themselves quite willing to use the fashionable catchwords of the moment, though they clearly believed in nothing but brute force; their methods, however, were different. Espartero rose by making himself the servant of the mob; Narvaez by obedience to an earnest though limited sense of duty; and O'Donnell by intrigue and open-eyed pursuit of self-aggrandizement. At the same time it should be said to the credit of Espartero that when, at the end of his life, he was offered the crown, he had the decency to refuse it.

By now Isabella had come of age, and it was clear that her reign would resemble the regency of her mother in all its essential details. There was the same desire on the part of the ruler to be absolute, and only to accept Liberal measures in the hope of being able to reverse them in the near future. The Queen's position in any case was not an easy one, for the traditions of government which had existed since the days of Ferdinand and Isabella had been rudely broken by the French invasion, and the restored absolutism had proved too inefficient when compared with that of Charles III to win men's minds back to the old ways. On the other hand, the Radicals and the growing republican party declared that in democracy alone would Spain find salvation, and as their remedy had never been tried it was hard to refute their argument.

Apathy of the Spaniards

Above all, there was the difficulty that the larger part of the population was politically apathetic, and those who took any interest in the government of their country were either Carlists or Radicals. Isabella had no principle upon which to base her rule, and there was no section of the community to which she was able to turn for support with any certainty of finding it, since the middle classes were hardly yet in existence, and those whose creed was 'Church and King' did not rally round her throne, but marched under the standard of Don Carlos. In these circumstances the monarchy was forced to rely on some chance grouping of factions in the Cortes, where the standard of ability in all parties was extremely low. As if this was not enough, the army was in a perpetual state of mutiny, and the generals thought more of seizing the reins of government than of enforcing discipline among their men. Isabella's position would thus in any case have been extremely difficult, but she rendered it hopeless by her scandalous method of living: the ancient Spanish loyalty to the royal line had been shaken by the Carlist movement, but the Queen came very near to destroying it altogether by her mode of life.

'The Spanish Marriages'

As soon as she reached marriageable age the question of selecting a suitable husband arose, and this produced the international crisis known as 'The Spanish Marriages' in 1846. Before Cristina ceased to be Regent it was her desire that her two daughters should each marry French princes, but it was pointed out by the powers, notably by Great Britain, that the Treaty of Utrecht was still in force, and that no close union between the crowns of France and Spain could be tolerated. After much negotiation the British government declared that it would have no objection to the marriage of Isabella's sister with the Duke of Montpensier, a son of the King of the French, once the Queen had married elsewhere than into the French Royal Family and had children of her own. Although an agreement was made between Paris and London on these lines, France did not keep to it, and the marriage of Isabella with her cousin Francis, reputed to be impotent, and that of her sister with Montpensier, were announced and celebrated at the same time. Once again the succession to the Spanish throne had international repercussions of the first magnitude, for the French King's breach of faith brought the recently formed Franco-British *Entente* to a sudden end, and this, in its turn, had much to do with the collapse of the French regime two years later. Nor was his ultimate ambition achieved, for Isabella soon produced the necessary heirs, among whom was the future Alfonso XII.

O'Donnell in Power

In the fifties and early sixties of the nineteenth century O'Donnell attempted to distract attention from the chaos at home by a spirited foreign policy. Yet though he might lead the army to victory in Morocco, re-incorporate Santo Domingo in the Spanish Empire, and send Spanish troops with those of France and Great Britain to Mexico, it availed him nothing, for at the end of five years of supreme power he was no nearer to establishing settled government in Spain. The whims of the Queen on the one hand, and the readiness of those politicians who were not in office to combine with disaffected military elements on the other, rendered stability impossible: the end came in the first weeks of 1863, when the Queen refused to assent to the recognition of the new Italian kingdom, and O'Donnell resigned.

The Revolution of 1868

The five years which followed saw the drift to chaos accelerated, and this was in no way slowed down by an unnecessary war with Chile and Peru, which brought to Spain neither honour nor victory. The financial situation also grew steadily worse, and there was a deficit of ten millions sterling. London and Paris refused any further help, and after an issue of bonds at 88 had failed, recourse was had to a forced loan: it cost fourteen million pounds to raise six million. The political situation was no better than the financial; one *pronunciamiento* succeeded another; the elections to the Cortes were carefully jerry-mandered; and the administration was falling into disorder: more dangerous to the regime was the fact that the various opposition parties began, as was again to be the case in 1930-1, to act together. Finally, in September 1868, the decisive blow was struck by a coalition of Republicans, Democrats, and Liberals, and the fleet, under the command of Admiral Topete, made a *pronunciamiento*. Its example was at once followed by various garrisons, and when the troops still loyal to the Queen failed, at a skirmish at Alcolea on the Guadalquivir, to check the insurrection, Isabella crossed the French frontier exclaiming, 'I thought I had struck deeper roots in this land'.

CHAPTER FIVE

Revolution and Restoration

The revolution of 1868 marked the end of old Spain. Isabella II and, before her, Cristina, had endeavoured to hold the balance even between it and the forces which had been unloosed by the French Revolution, and for which the way had to no inconsiderable extent been paved by the earlier Bourbons. Circumstances, due almost entirely to the Carlist split, had been too much for them, and henceforth, almost down to our own time, the destinies of the country were to be in the hands of those who, whatever the regime, based their rule upon a set of ideas that were, not Spanish, but foreign, in their origin.

Search for a King

The victorious revolutionaries, like Napoleon sixty years before, soon discovered that it was easier to overthrow the Bourbons than to find anything durable to put in their place. There were few, except the great orator Emilio Castelar, who yet wanted a republic, and as there was no suitable Spaniard to fill the vacancy the crown was hawked round Europe. It was refused by the Portuguese royal family, and then, on second thoughts, by Prince Leopold of Hohenzollern, though the fact that he had toyed with the offer was one of the causes of the Franco-Prussian War – yet another instance of Spanish affairs producing a European crisis. Finally, in 1870, a monarch was found in Amadeo, Duke of Aosta, a young son of King Victor Emmanual II of Italy. The fates, however, were against him from the beginning, for, on the very day that he landed in the Peninsula, General Prim, who had been chiefly instrumental in persuading him to accept the throne, was murdered in Madrid.

Amadeo

Amadeo was honest and courageous to a degree, and he was prepared to sacrifice himself in the interests of his adopted country, but the Spaniards would have none of him. To them he was an intruder – *el rey intruso* – as Joseph Bonaparte had been. To the more religiously minded he was abhorrent as the son of the man who had despoiled the Pope of his temporal power; the more frivolous *Madrileños* mocked his Italian accent; the aristocracy ridiculed his Piedmontese austerity; and the Republicans were impatient at the presence of a man who seemed by his very virtues to postpone the realization of their dream. Above all, the Carlists received an enormous accession of strength now that the other branch of the Royal House was under a cloud, and had they played their cards properly they should have won the day at this time. In these circumstances Amadeo never had a chance, and his only supporters were a handful of adventurers who had no thoughts but to fill their pockets before the inevitable crash.

The new King struggled on for two years, and when the end came it was due to a minor issue connected with the artillery. That branch of the Spanish forces had always been exclusive, and promotion from the ranks was unknown. The serjeants of this arm had taken part in a meeting in 1866, and one of the senior officers, a General Hidalgo, had for political reasons sided with the mutineers, thereby not unnaturally earning the cordial dislike of his brother-officers. On the advice of Ruiz Zorrilla, the Prime Minister, Amadeo appointed Hidalgo to the Captaincy-General of Catalonia, whereupon the artillery officers who were serving against the Carlists on that front resigned their commissions by way of protest. Ruiz Zorrilla accepted the challenge, the artillery corps was formally dissolved, and non-commissioned officers were appointed to fill the vacancies. Although Amadeo did not approve of matters being pushed to such extremes, he signed the necessary decrees, but he took advantage of the opportunity to abdicate. In a dignified message to the Cortes he pointed out that the misfortunes of Spain were due to the Spaniards themselves, and on 12 February 1873 he left the country. Typical of the calibre of the Spanish politician of that day was the fact that among the documents which he did not sign before his departure, although presented for his signature, was one conferring the Golden Fleece upon Ruiz Zorrilla.

The First Republic

As soon as the abdication of Amadeo became known the two Chambers quite unconstitutionally coalesced into a National Assembly, and proclaimed a Republic by 258 votes to 32, with one Figueras as President. By this time the state of the country was going from bad to worse: the northern provinces, except the towns, were in the hands of the Carlists, Andalusia had relapsed into anarchy, and Catalonia was, for all practical purposes, independent. Nor were the Republicans united among themselves, for they were divided into those who wished Spain to be a federal, and those who would have her a unitary state: the leaders of the respective parties were Pi y Margall and Salmerón. In a country in which centrifugal influences had always been strong, and where the monarchy no longer existed to check them, the federal idea made an effective appeal, and it was not long before the extreme federalists, particularly in Andalusia, began to preach *Cantonalismo*, or a constitution based on that of Switzerland.

Anarchy in the Peninsula

The First Republic started badly, for Figueras, appalled by the difficulties of his position, fled the country without even the formality of a resignation, and Pi y Margall took his place. While, however, the Government was considering the question of dividing Spain into thirteen semi-independent states, the very foundations of civilized society were giving way: perhaps the best description of the position was that of the most convinced Republican of them all, namely Castelar:

We are now witnessing what I never imagined we would live to see. Daily riots, general strife, and military indiscipline have everywhere been let loose. Our colleagues are being killed in the streets of towns that a short time ago were peaceful, and that are now a prey to the power of revolt. There is a demagogic dictatorship in Cadiz, and civil war in Malaga is causing half the population to abandon the city. The garrison has been disarmed at Granada, and bands of insurgents set out from one town, without aim or reason, in order to fight and perish in another. We have arson and murder at Alcoy, anarchy at Valencia, and brigandage in Sierra Morena. Murcia is in the hands of the demagogues, and Castellon has fallen to the reactionaries. The villagers of Castille erect barricades in their streets and declare war upon each other. Seville is up in arms, the people of Cartagena are the victims of a delirious frenzy, and Alicante and Almería have been bombarded. The Spanish fleet alternately hoists a red flag and a foreign banner.

In respect of this last charge of Castelar, it is interesting to note that the British Navy finally took possession of the Spanish ships to prevent their crews embarking upon a piractical career, and interned them at Gibraltar.

The widespread anarchy compelled the resignation of Pi y Margall, and his place was taken by Salmerón: he showed more energy than his predecessor, and sent General Pavia to restore order in Andalusia, but after two months he, too, was compelled to resign, and gave place to Castelar. This statesman had not long been in office before he incurred the hostility of the majority in the Cortes on account of the rigorous methods, such as the revival of conscription, to which he was driven in order to re-establish a respect for the law. As it was clear that the deputies would not support Castelar much longer, Pavia determined to save the President in spite of himself, and so he executed a *coup d'etat* in January 1874. Castelar, however, refused to owe power to military support, and he was succeeded in office by General Ramón Serrano, who naturally had no such scruples.

Another Carlist War

The twelve months that followed were occupied by the struggle against the Carlists, who on one occasion came within striking distance of Madrid itself. There had been more than one Carlist rising, notably in 1846 and 1848, since the first Don Carlos had been compelled to abandon the fight, and in 1860 two of the Carlist princes had been captured during an abortive attempt in Catalonia. The proclamation of the First Republic rekindled Carlist enthusiasm. The Carlist heir arrived in the Peninsula in due course, and had he possessed a capable statesman and a competent general he must have won; but for various reasons, not least because of the savagery of his followers, which he was unable to check, he never succeeded in recapturing in himself the growing anti-republican feelings in the country; for in spite of the fact that the Republic had succeeded in holding the Carlists at bay, and that under Serrano there was relative order, its credit was steadily declining. On 31 December 1873, the 3 per cent Exterior Debt had already fallen on the London Stock Exchange to 17¼, and the coupons on this issue remained unpaid for eighteen months, having to be refunded by the government of the Restoration.

Restoration of Alfonso XII

Meanwhile, new men were coming to the fore in Spanish politics, and among them on the Right was Cánovas del Castillo, who was quietly preparing for the advent of a

Liberal monarchy in the person of Isabella's son, the Prince of the Asturias. Cánovas wished to restore the monarchy in a peaceful manner, and above all else to avoid the intervention of the military. Most unfortunately for the future course of Spanish history he was unable to effect his purpose, for in December 1874, General Martinez Campos made a monarchist *pronunciamiento*, and his example was speedily followed by the other army commanders. On 9 January 1875, Alfonso XII reached Barcelona, and the world testified its approval by a rise of four points in Spanish funds.

Defeat of the Carlists

The first task of the restored monarchy was to crush the Carlist risings. The Restoration had in itself proved that Don Carlos had finally missed his chance, and it also deprived him of many who were prepared to accept him as the only method of overturning the Republic, while the Pope's recognition of Alfonso XII weakened his position with the clergy and with no inconsiderable section of the laity. All through the year 1875 the Carlists were steadily pushed back, but it was not until the beginning of 1876 that Primo de Rivera succeeded in capturing Estella, their headquarters. In March of that year Don Carlos was obliged to cross the frontier, and the Second Carlist War was over. The Basques lost their centuries-old *Fueros*, or special rights, but they were accorded certain privileges in the matter of taxation: yet, if Carlism had been defeated in the field its spirit survived.

A New Constitution

It was not until March 1876 that the new constitution was brought forward by Cánovas in the Cortes, and it was to a large extent modelled upon that of Great Britain. Legislation was vested in a Cortes of two chambers with the King, and the chambers were of equal authority. The Senate consisted of eighty senators in their own right, a hundred nominated by the Crown, and 180 elected by local bodies, the universities, and taxpayers of the highest class: one-half of the elected senators was renewed every fifth year. The Chamber was elected by districts of 50,000 inhabitants, but it was not until 1890 that there was adult suffrage, and even then the vote was limited to men; there was also, in the larger towns, a form of proportional representation. The King alone had the right to summon, prorogue, or dissolve the Cortes, but a dissolution had to be followed by the assembly of a new one within three months. Finally, the King was irresponsible, but his decrees had to be countersigned by a responsible minister.

This constitution remained in force until the establishment of the Directory in 1923. Theoretically it left little to be desired, but in the last resort it depended for successful working upon the willing co-operation of the Spanish people, and this condition was never fulfilled. Cánovas himself did not believe that his fellow-countrymen were ready for such a constitution, but he hoped that with the passage of time it would take root; in this he was disappointed, for what happened was that the political life of Spain became a hollow sham. There were two main parties in the Cortes, the Conservatives and the Liberals, led respectively by Cánovas and Sagasta, and they alternated in office as parties of the same name were doing in contemporary Britain. The elections were shamelessly 'made' in order to give a majority to one side or the other, for the two leaders were working together to ensure that there should be an outward appearance of normal constitutional life. So long as Cánovas and Sagasta lived this illusion was sustained, but when they died the parties began to break up into groups, and as the system had no secure foundations it was very soon completely undermined.

Its Weaknesses

The end at which Cánovas aimed may, or may not, have justified the means which he employed to achieve it, but the means remained long after the end had been forgotten, and they were the 'making' of the elections. The vast majority of the electorate was unable to read or write, and power in the constituencies was in the hands of the *cacique*, who resembled the 'boss' of American politics. The corruption which this system produced can easily be imagined, and it extended to the local authorities as well. During the course of an enquiry held in the 1920s by order of the Directory, for example, it was found that in Murcia there had been no entry in the day-books or ledgers of the municipality for years; in Orense the windows of the local hospital were never mended; and in Palencia there was no heating in the local maternity hospital, although it was 3,000 feet above sea-level. Such examples might be multiplied indefinitely, and all over Spain only a small proportion of the money voted for any particular purpose ever reached it. There was no awakening of the national consciousness to these abuses, though it must be stressed that the personal honesty of the ordinary Spaniard remained uncontaminated by the venality of his politicians.

Early Death of Alfonso XII

Alfonso XII died on 25 November 1885 at the early age of twenty-eight. On the whole Spain had been quieter during his reign than at any time since the Napoleonic invasion. It is true that he was, unlike his mother and his son, fortunate in his ministers, especially Cánovas and Sagasta, but he had the good sense to appreciate their worth. He found Spain in a state of chaos – moral, social, and political, and he left her at peace, making considerable material progress; so that he well deserved his title of *El Pacificador*, and the equestrian statue which towers over the lake in the Retiro at Madrid.

The Cuban Complication

The shadow of Cuba fell over the short reign of Alfonso XII and the earlier of his son's years. That island, with Puerto Rico, was all that remained of the Spanish dominions in the Americas, and since 1868 it had been the scene of a savage war to obtain independence. Before the First

Republic fell there were 100,000 troops in Cuba; at the opening of his first Cortes the King said that 32,000 more had been sent there; and in 1877 Martinez Campos went out at the head of another 14,000: yet the insurgents were only a few thousand strong. It was a foretaste of the Vietnam war of more recent times. Service in the island was universally unpopular, for only a small proportion of those who went to Cuba ever returned to Spain, so heavy a toll of life was taken by the climate. Martinez Campos succeeded in effecting a pacification in 1878 by giving way upon every important point, but the Treaty of El Zanjón, which satisfied neither loyalists nor separatists, was a mere truce.

It settled nothing, and as the years passed it became abundantly clear that with one or two honourable exceptions, such as Antonio Maura, the politicians had no intention of meeting even the more moderate demands of those who were advocating a redress of the island's grievances. The truth was that Cuba was a closely-protected market for dear and bad Catalan goods, while its administration contained numerous lucrative sinecures to which the friends and relatives of influential deputies might be appointed. In 1895 the struggle broke out afresh, and Martinez Campos was once more sent to deal with the situation. He proved unable to effect any improvement, and was superseded by General Weyler, who adopted a method of warfare that shocked the conscience of the nineteenth century. The U.S. Congress discussed a motion calling upon the President to mediate, while, to add to the embarrassment of the Spanish Government, an insurrection broke out in the Philippines. At this critical moment the country was deprived of the services of its ablest statesman, for in 1897 Cánovas, like Prim before, and Canalejas and Dato after him, was murdered.

War with the United States

During the winter of 1897–8 the tension between Spain and the United States became steadily greater. The American press, acting as the mouthpiece of the armament firms and other vested interests that wanted war, whipped up its readers to a fine patriotic frenzy, and there was a long series of 'incidents'. Finally, in February 1898, the U.S. cruiser *Maine* was destroyed by an explosion in the harbour of Havana, and the Spanish suggestion of an impartial inquiry into the cause of the disaster was rejected by President McKinley. An ultimatum was sent to Spain demanding the evacuation of Cuba, and the reply was a declaration of war on 14 April 1898.

The Spanish naval and military forces were quite inadequate to operate against a powerful enemy so far from the Peninsula, and in what was, for the most part, hostile territory. The first act of the Americans was to blockade Havana and the north coast of Cuba. Admiral Cervera was sent from Spain to raise the blockade, and he made his base at Santiago. The American army therefore proceeded to invest Santiago by land, and this forced Cervera to put to sea: in the fight which followed all his ships were sunk, burnt, run ashore, or captured, and a fortnight later Santiago surrendered. Meanwhile, the Spanish forces were no more successful in the Philippines, where Admiral Dewey was in charge of the American operations. In both theatres, however, the Spaniards fought with great gallantry, while the Americans were assisted to no inconsiderable extent by the insurgents. By July it was clear that Spain could no longer continue the struggle, and after fruitless efforts to negotiate terms of peace, she was obliged to accept those dictated by her victorious opponents: they proved to be the surrender of Cuba, Puerto Rico, and the Philippines. In return Spain received from the United States an indemnity of four million pounds, which was paid as a result of pressure upon Washington by the international armament firms, who feared that otherwise she might be unable to discharge her debts to them.

The 'Generation of 1898'

The loss of her best overseas possessions was a severe blow to the pride of Spain, and for many years 1898 was regarded as a turning-point in her history: we now know that such was not the case. Had her statesmen taken advantage of what had happened to concentrate upon the internal improvement of their country, the disaster of the war might have proved to be a blessing in disguise, but they did no such thing. The generals who had proved unable to save Cuba and the Philippines found their influence at home in no way diminished. There was not even a change of ministry in consequence of the catastrophe, and before many years the incompetence of the administration made of Morocco another Cuba, where Spanish lives and money were poured out like water. It is true that there came into existence a literary school, called somewhat grandiloquently the 'Generation of 1898', of which 'Azorin', Unamuno, and Baroja were the outstanding figures, and that it marked a reaction against the standards of the preceding period. All over Europe, however, the same forces were at work, and it is nothing more than a coincidence that in Spain the new spirit in literature should have been contemporary with the loss of the colonies. It would have been well for Spain had that event marked a turning point in her history, but this did not happen.

The Regency of Maria Cristina

Alfonso XII had left his widow, Maria Cristina of Austria, with two daughters, and about to give birth to another child. The nation at once gave proof of the innate chivalry of the Spanish character by rallying round the Queen, who became Regent on her husband's death, and so both Carlists and Republicans found themselves deprived of the opportunity to make trouble. On 17 May 1886, the new monarch, Alfonso XIII, was born, and it was due to the courage and ability of his mother that the early years of his reign were so peaceful. When Alfonso XII died Maria Cristina was little more than a name to the Spanish people, but she soon won a place in their hearts which she never lost. Unfortunately, the political truce which marked her regency had certain unhappy repercussions, for it made stagnation the order of the day. The laudable determination to avoid a crisis resulted in a tendency not to do anything at all, and thus Spain drifted, quite unprepared, into the catastrophe of war with the United States.

Alfonso XIII

In 1902 the regency came to an end, and the young King entered upon his inheritance. Unhappily for him there was no one to take the place of Cánovas, nor in whom he could trust. The parties were already breaking up into groups, and with each ministerial crisis the formation of a new administration became more difficult. There were, it is true, a few outstanding men, notably Maura, Canalejas, Dato, and Villaverde, but they never enjoyed the prestige or influence of Cánovas and Sagasta. The consequence was that the King had to interfere in the details of government to prevent the whole machinery of administration from coming to a standstill, and in this way he learned to play one politician off against another. To a certain extent this was necessary in the interests of the country as a whole, but it now became a habit to the monarch, and in the end he was widely distrusted on that score in political circles. Yet from the first he showed himself a patriotic Spaniard, and his intelligence was above the level of most of his ministers – a fact which did not improve his relations with them.

Disintegration of the Political System

The period from 1902 until the outbreak of the First World War witnessed the progressive disintegration of the political system established at the Restoration. One transient ministry followed another, until in 1910 the Liberals came into office under Canalejas, one of the few really able Spanish statesmen of the present century. His programme included the reform of education, increased expenditure on health and public works, and stricter control of the Church. This provoked widespread opposition, but the King stood by his minister, and it looked as if the reform of the State was going to be accomplished at last. In 1912, however, Canalejas was murdered, and things went on as before. Personalities, not principles, divided the politicians, and succeeding administrations were so dependent, in the absence of an educated public opinion, upon vested interests, national and local, that nothing was ever done.

Revolutionary Activity

It was the more unfortunate that the parliamentary system should break down at this time, for extremist doctrines were beginning to gain ground, notably in Barcelona. The murder of Canalejas was only an incident in the anarchist campaign that marked the closing years of last century, for in 1906 a peculiarly dastardly attempt was made to murder the King in the streets of Madrid on the day of his marriage to Princess Victoria Eugénie of Battenburg. Three years later the storm broke, and for a space there was civil war in Barcelona and its neighbourhood. The instigator of what would today be termed a Communist rising was one Francisco Ferrer, a militant atheist of considerable ability, passionate conviction, and loose morals. After some hard fighting, in which much damage was done, the revolt was suppressed, and Maura, who was Prime Minister at the time, refused to prevent Ferrer's execution: Ferrer thereupon became a martyr in the eyes of the extreme Left. This insurrection showed that the old anarchical spirit in Spain was still alive, and that when the governmental system was weakening it would, as in so many previous instances, prove a menace of the very first magnitude.

The First World War

Such was the unsatisfactory state of affairs when the First World War broke out in 1914. Although Spain quite rightly maintained her neutrality to the end, the conflict had a tremendous influence upon her. It brought her riches which she had not known since the wealth of the Indies had been brought to her shores in the sixteenth century, and whole districts were industrialized almost overnight to supply the demands of the belligerents. Stock of all kinds attained unheard-of prices, and if Spain did not become a creditor country she was able to buy out the foreign investor in most Spanish enterprises, such as the Andaluces railway. At the same time, this wave of prosperity increased the growing dissatisfaction with the governmental machine, for the politicians proved quite incapable of taking advantage of what was happening to initiate a real national revival. They continued to play the old wearisome game of 'ins' and 'outs', with never a thought to the chances they were missing of setting their country on its feet again for all time. The suppression of the troubles in Barcelona had been forgotten, and revolutionary strikes were frequent. Equally ominous was the formation at this time of *juntas* of officers to act as guardians of the army's interests, for this foreshadowed a return to the days of the *pronunciamiento*.

Contemporary with the ending of the First World War was the last attempt of the parliamentary system, in the person of the Liberal-Conservative Dato, to redress the grievances of Spain. The eight-hour day was established in 1919, for Dato realized that most of the troubles of his fellow-countrymen were economic and social, rather than political. Bills were passed dealing with workmen's insurance, compensation for accidents, and the regulation of women's and children's work, and it looked as if Spain had at last found a leader, but then, in March 1921, Dato, too, was murdered. He and Canalejas, alone among the successors of Cánovas and Sagasta, could have infused new life into the Constitution of 1876. Indeed, Dato had not long been in his grave before events took place in Morocco which brought the whole edifice crashing to the ground.

The War in the Riff

By the Algeciras Conference in 1906 France and Spain were given a free hand in Morocco, and in due course they divided the country into two zones of influence: in this division France was definitely the gainer, for Spain was merely entrusted with a strip of the north coast, which included the mountains of the Riff with the fierce tribesmen who inhabited them. In the spring of 1921 two Spanish armies were endeavouring to bring them to order when the rashness of the commander, General Silvestre, of one of them led to a crushing defeat with heavy losses both in men and material. It is true that the lost territory was recovered by General Berenguer before the end of the year, but the damage to Spanish prestige was not so easily repaired.

The Pronunciamiento of General Primo de Rivera

The effect of this disaster in Spain itself was to drive the last nail into the coffin of the parliamentary system, for rightly or wrongly public opinion laid the blame, not upon the soldiers, but upon the politicians in Madrid. Unhappily the country at this time was also suffering severely from the disorders attendant upon feeble administration. All the native anarchy of the race came to the surface, and there were repeated revolutionary strikes, attended with bloodshed. Communist emissaries would appear at a factory, and compel those employed there to cease work without giving any reason for their action, and such was the terror they inspired that they were rarely disobeyed. Murders were perpetrated with impunity, and even on the rare occasions when the culprits were caught, no jury could be found to convict. In June 1923, the disorders reached their climax in the brutal assassination of the Cardinal Archbishop of Zaragoza. Three months later, on 13 September, General Primo de Rivera, then Captain-General of Catalonia, made his *pronunciamiento*, and received such widespread support that the ministers made no opposition. The military Directory then came into existence, and what proved to be the final break with the Constitution of 1876 took place.

CHAPTER SIX

The Directory and the Second Republic

The head of the Directory was Miguel Primo de Rivera, Marquis of Estella, a man of fifty-three with a distinguished military career behind him. In fact he was a soldier above all else: that was both his strength and his weakness. The impression which he made upon those who came into contact with him was that of a man absolutely sincere, and prepared to make any personal sacrifice for what he believed to be right. He was also completely fearless, and he walked about the streets of Madrid in the same careless way after he had seized power as he did before that event. A true aristocrat, he deliberately avoided all ostentation, and when he returned to the capital after his victorious campaign in Africa, he entered it as a private citizen. When he went to his club or to a theatre, in nine cases out of ten his presence was unknown. There was also an unfailing courtesy about him which one could not fail to perceive, and at a critical moment in the Moroccan campaign he found time to write a letter of thanks to an English lady who had sent him a message of congratulation.

The King and the Dictator

Unfortunately, there was another side to the picture, and this proved in the end to be the undoing both of himself and of Spain. Like so many soldiers, Primo de Rivera recognized only two colours, black and white, but in politics the distinction is rarely as clear as that. With the passage of time and the emergence of fresh problems, social and economic, with which his early training had not equipped him to deal, he got out of his depth; and that is the explanation of the blunders which marked the later years of his tenure of office. He estranged all the old politicians, the best of whom would otherwise have helped him, and his relations with the King were never good. In these circumstances Primo de Rivera became increasingly more isolated, and only a genius, which he was not, can afford to stand alone.

At the same time there can be no shadow of doubt but that the *pronunciamiento*, and the closing of the Cortes which followed it, were exceedingly popular: had a plebiscite been taken the Directory would have obtained an overwhelming majority. The fact that the change had been effected by the army in no way disturbed public opinion, for Spain had become accustomed to military intervention in politics, and the army was at this period probably more representative of the country than was the Cortes. The General himself never lost his popularity with the masses, however much the middle classes and the intellectuals might sneer at him, and the King's apparently callous treatment of him after his fall undoubtedly contributed not a little to undermine the monarch's own position.

Establishment of the Directory

When the *pronunciamiento* was made at Barcelona the King was at San Sebastian, and he hurried back to Madrid, where he met the then Prime Minister and the other members of the Cabinet. The ministers confessed their inability to control the situation, for all the garrisons had announced their support of Primo de Rivera, and resigned. The King had thus no choice but to accept a military Directory, and it is impossible to censure him for the action which he took at this exceedingly difficult moment. Where he did make a mistake was in not insisting upon the convocation of the Cortes, within the three months prescribed by the

12 *The cross in the Valle de los Caidos in Cuelgamuros*

13 *Street scene in Madrid today*

constitution, to sanction what had been done. Had this course been adopted the General could easily have obtained from the Cortes not only the ratification of what had happened, but a completely free hand in the future: in that event, the charge of being unconstitutional, later to be used against the monarch with such damning effect, could never have been made. King Alfonso considered that the constitution was suspended, and such was the case, but, as it contained no provision for its temporary suspension, he was, in law, acting in an unconstitutional manner. Of course, the constitution had so often been disregarded in the past that one more breach of it did not seem to matter, but on this occasion it was to place a very effective weapon in the hands of the enemies of the throne.

The Moroccan Campaign

The first task of the Directory was to re-establish respect for the law, and this was speedily accomplished by a few exemplary sentences on wrongdoers, but its preoccupation was Morocco. There the Moors, under the leadership of Abd-el-Krim, had invaded the French zone, and it became obvious that joint Franco-Spanish action alone could check them. In July 1925, the representatives of France and Spain met in Madrid, and at a subsequent interview between Primo de Rivera and Marshal Pétain the actual plan of campaign was settled. On 8 September, under the supreme command of Primo de Rivera and covered by the fire of the Franco–Spanish fleet, the Spaniards landed in Alhucemas Bay, and stormed the surrounding heights with the greatest gallantry. Then followed a month's hard fighting, and Abd-el-Krim's capital, Ajdir, was captured. Even that did not put an end to the war, for the Moors unsuccessfully attempted negotiation. When hostilities were resumed General Sanjurjo inflicted a heavy defeat on the Moors, and by the late spring of 1926 the war was at an end, although the final pacification of the Spanish zone occupied a few months more.

Home Policy

The victorious termination of the Moroccan campaign enormously enhanced the prestige of the Directory. Originally it had been composed exclusively of generals and admirals, but in December 1925, it was remodelled with the addition of such distinguished civilians as Calvo Sotelo, at the Ministry of Finance, and the Count of Guadalhorce, at the Ministry of Public Works. Looking at the work of the Directory in retrospect there can be no gainsaying the fact that in the six years of its existence it did more for Spain than had been effected in the previous sixty. Great progress was made in the matter of hydro-electric development by the establishment of autonomous corporations, each of which controlled one of the great river-basins of the country. Contracts were given out for the construction of nearly 400 miles of railway and over 4,000 miles of road, while the telephone service was entirely reorganized by the Compañia Telefónica Nacional. The problem of financial reform was also attacked at its root by drastic changes in the system of taxation. The military and naval authorities, too, distinguished themselves this year by the organization of Commandante Franco's flight to South America, and by a no less successful one from Madrid to the Philippines. Both these events encouraged interest in the possibilities of aviation, and were made an occasion for a reaffirmation of Hispano-American friendship.

The Catalan Problem

On the other hand a serious blunder was made by the Directory in its handling of the Catalan problem. As in the not dissimilar case of Ireland a little autonomy at the beginning would have prevented virtual independence in the end. The King of Spain was also Count of Barcelona, and much use might have been made of this fact, but Primo de Rivera set his face against any policy that savoured of concession. Yet the more moderate section of Catalan opinion, which was alarmed at the friendly relations existing between such extreme separatists as Colonel

Macia and the Communists, would have welcomed co-operation with Madrid on any terms that recognized their point of view. The result of the government's obduracy was to throw the Catalans into the arms of the Republicans and Socialists in opposition, first to the Directory, and eventually to the monarchy itself. It was suicidal, and totally unnecessary.

The Directory in Decline

The year 1926, which witnessed the triumph of the Directory, also marked the commencement of its decline, and from then onwards nothing seemed to go right. Spain failed to obtain a permanent seat on the Council of the League of Nations; there was trouble in the armed forces; and martial law had to be proclaimed all over the country; so in spite of the benefits which the Directory were conferring, every passing day showed ever more clearly how difficult it is to reform a nation from above. The Government itself soon began to feel this, and in 1927 a National Assembly was convoked to replace the Cortes: the deputies were to some extent representative of various corporations, but they had no legislative power, and all that was effected by calling this body into existence was to prove that the Directory did not feel sure of its position, for the National Assembly was never regarded as anything more than a rather poor joke. Primo de Rivera was also decidedly unfortunate in his dealings with the intellectual classes, and the harsh treatment which was too often meted out to men of international reputation created the worst possible impression abroad. A further blunder was the favour which was shown to the regular clergy, particularly in the matter of teaching, for this irritated their old rivals, the seculars, and also enraged lay educationalists.

Fall of the Directory

In 1929 there took place magnificent exhibitions at Barcelona and Seville, but they proved to be the swansong of the Directory. The General's health was obviously giving way beneath the strain to which it was subjected; an extravagant economic nationalism had sent up the cost of living; and repeated conspiracies were being discovered by the police. At the beginning of 1930 Primo de Rivera, ill and wearied, committed the crowning blunder of violating the King's prerogative by asking the various Captains-General whether they thought he should remain in office. This left the monarch no choice but to dismiss his minister, and it is very much to the latter's credit that he was the first to admit the mistake he had made. A few weeks afterwards he died in a Paris hotel, and the fact that King Alfonso was not present at his subsequent funeral in Madrid told heavily against the Crown.

The King's Choice

The fall of the Directory left Alfonso face to face with the opponents of his late ministry and there were many people who censured the monarch more than the General, for they held that whereas the King had sworn to observe the constitution Primo de Rivera had assumed no such liability. The situation was one of peculiar difficulty for the old Conservative and Liberal parties had been reduced to mere shadows, and all that remained of them were their erstwhile leaders, whom events soon proved to carry no weight at all: on the other hand the Socialists and Communists had gained considerable ground, and their organizations were intact, if subterranean. The King then decided that the safest course would be to return to normalcy at the earliest possible moment, and he charged General Berenguer to form a government for this purpose. Thereupon there ensued two troubled years, during which the political situation went from bad to worse, while for one reason or another elections were continually being postponed, while the Left gained in strength every day by asserting that the Government never intended to hold them at all. Finally, in February 1931, Berenguer resigned, and was replaced by Admiral Aznar: it was the beginning of the end.

The constitution of the new administration made revolution inevitable, for it marked the return to power of those very politicians whom the vast majority of Spaniards, whatever their political opinions, hoped the Directory had driven out of public life for ever. Now they had returned at the King's request, and from the moment they took office the fate of the throne was sealed. Even the most convinced monarchists had no desire to fight for those whom they profoundly distrusted, while the ministers themselves had no sort of following in the country. The issue had become narrowed to a vote for or against the Crown, and all the advantages were with the opponents of the latter. They had managed, partly by their own skill but chiefly owing to the blunders of Berenguer, to unite against the monarchy all those who had disapproved of the Directory, all those who had lost their jobs under the administration of its successor, and all who were determined to prevent the government falling once more into the hands of the old politicians. It was a masterpiece of political strategy, though this cannot disguise the fact that had King Alfonso possessed reasonably competent advisers it would have failed.

Collapse of the Monarchy

Admiral Aznar and his colleagues decided to hold the local elections first, and to do this on 12 April 1931, but before that date two events took place which well illustrate the incurable levity of the Spaniard of those days in matters political. The Queen returned from a visit to England, and both at the station in Madrid and during their passage through the streets she and her husband were greeted with the most tumultuous enthusiasm. A week before the election was Easter Sunday, and the elaborate ceremonial associated with that event at the Spanish Court was carried out without a hitch, in the midst of popular approval. The Spaniard was apparently quite ready to acclaim the King one day and to vote Republican the next, so that in the circumstances it is hardly surprising that no power abroad, with the exception of the Holy See, should have foreseen what was about to happen.

The elections were duly held on 12 April, and of the councillors returned no less than 22,150 were Monarchists as against 5,875 Republicans. With the exception of the four Catalan provinces, Huesca, and Vizcaya, the result was wholly favourable to the existing order, but the Republicans carried all the large towns save Cadiz, Palma de Mallorca, and Pamplona. For the King this was naturally a severe shock, and he said, 'I had the impression of calling on an old friend and finding him dead'. The elections had, of course, no competence where the regime was concerned, and the voting was a warning that it did not want the old politicians back in office, but nothing more. The ministers, however, lost their heads, and Admiral Aznar went so far as to declare to the press that the country had gone Republican overnight.

Departure of King Alfonso XIII

In effect, the monarchy was not overthrown; it collapsed, as in 1868. When the results of the elections became known the Republicans in Madrid began to demonstrate, and as the authorities did nothing to stop them they became bolder every hour. The King realized that the monarchy could at this stage be saved only by bloodshed, but, to his credit he refused to order the troops to fire upon his subjects. The Republican leaders, for their part, were only anxious to take advantage of the existing situation to get the Royal Family out of Spain before there was a revulsion of feeling in its favour. In consequence, King Alfonso departed by way of Cartagena, and the Queen and her children by that of Irun. The victorious Republicans were in such a hurry to see the monarch on foreign soil that he was able to leave Spain without signing any deed of abdication.

The Second Republic

The most notable fact about the advent to power of the Second Republic was thus the ease with which it took place, and this had no little connection with its ultimate undoing. In no quarter was there the slightest opposition. The Royalists might have utilized their strength in the countryside to embarrass the new rulers of Spain, but they did nothing of the sort: they were too dazed to act, while their complete lack of a leader, once the King had gone, was a further handicap. It must also be confessed that at this moment there was, owing to the events of the previous decade, little enthusiasm for Alfonso XIII, in whom the cause of monarchism was personified. It was, too, believed, with that facile optimism which always attends the morrow of a revolution, that the change which had occurred must necessarily be for the better: even on the Right it was taken for granted that the Republic would be a very moderate affair, which all save the extreme die-hards would be able to support.

This state of affairs certainly enabled the victorious Republicans to assume control with the minimum of inconvenience to themselves, but it was soon to be a serious embarrassment. The revolutionaries were, as has been shown, composed of different elements, and the one thing that might have welded them together would have been a hard fight against a common enemy. This they never had, and the resulting weakness soon became apparent. The last years of the monarchy witnessed the formation by the Pact of San Sebastian of a coalition of Radicals, Socialists, and Catalan autonomists, while the history of the Second Republic was to be that of the disintegration of the coalition with civil war as the ultimate consequence.

Its Basic Weakness

The Spanish Revolution of 1931 suffered from the further disadvantage of being in many ways an anachronism. Its leaders proved themselves in only too many cases to be men with a nineteenth-century outlook, and they were thus in conflict with the spirit of their age, which was variously interpreted as Fascist or Communist, but which was certainly not in sympathy with *bourgeois* Liberalism, or even with conventional Socialism; yet these were the forms of government which the victorious revolutionaries were, for the most part, pledged to establish. Without casting any reflection upon the motives of the leading Spanish Republicans it is impossible to resist the conclusion that they were living in the world of 1848, and the course of events which led up to the fall of the monarchy is certainly reminiscent of an earlier age. The Second Republic did not introduce any fresh ideas of government, and no revolution is worthy of the name which has not a spiritual as well as a material aspect. This was not, however, apparent in the spring of 1931, save to a few foreign observers, and the change of regime was generally interpreted as a step forward along the path of progress.

The Provisional Government which was constituted on the fall of the monarchy contained representatives of the various groups which had been parties to the Pact of San Sebastian with Alcalá Zamora, an old monarchist, as Prime Minister. Its first task was to solve the problem of Catalonia, which was done by constituting that province into what a British lawyer would have described as a more or less autonomous body with a status somewhere between that of a colony, with an unofficial majority in the legislature, and a dominion. The immediate effect, however, was to whet the appetite for self-government of other regions of Spain where centrifugal influences were still powerful.

Anti-Clerical Policy

After satisfying the demands of their Catalan allies in this way, the ministers decided not to embark upon any far-reaching changes until a Cortes had been elected. This at once roused the hostility of the extremists who had not gone into the streets merely to put Alcalá Zamora in the place of King Alfonso, and they determined to force the hand of the Government. As the monarchy was gone, the most prominent representative of the old order was the Church, and in May 1931, the storm against her broke all over Spain. Convents and churches were sacked and burnt, while the police made no attempt to interfere. In many districts the inhabitants, once they realized that those who were nominally responsible for the preservation of law and order intended to do nothing, banded themselves together in defence of the clergy and their property, and thus put a stop to the perpetration of fresh excesses; while elsewhere the outrages ceased only when there were no more religious buildings to be gutted. Some idea of the damage can be gained from the fact that in Malaga alone nearly fifty churches were sacked; in Madrid libraries containing upwards of 135,000 books were destroyed; while many valuable pictures, including at least one Titian, perished in the flames in different parts of the country.

Elections and a New Constitution

The elections for the Cortes were held at the end of June, and they resulted in the return of an overwhelming majority of deputies pledged to support the Republic. Indeed, the majority was far too large, for it soon began to break up, while it was a genuine misfortune for Spain that the Right, which was beginning to gather force in the country under the leadership of Gil Robles, should hardly have been represented at all. The first sign of this reaction was at a by-election in Madrid in the autumn, when José Antonio Primo de Rivera, son of the late Marquis of Estella, stood as a candidate of the Right, and halved the previous Socialist majority. In October there was a disagreement in the Cabinet between the moderates and the extremists, and a partial reconstruction of the ministry took place in consequence.

The new constitution made its appearance at the end of the year, and it proved to be essentially a Liberal document, though the influence of the Socialists was obvious in many of its provisions. Government was vested in the President and one Chamber, and in due course

Alcalá Zamora was elected to the Presidency of the
Republic, while Manuel Azaña, a man of the Left, became
Prime Minister at the head of a Cabinet which was pre-
dominantly Radical-Socialist and Socialist in its com-
position. At the same time there was enacted a law for the
defence of the Republic which conferred such arbitrary
powers on the Government as largely to neutralize the
Liberal provisions of the constitution of which it formed
part.

Progressive Disintegration of the Left

The enactment of the constitution and the formation of
the Azaña administration brought to a close what may be
termed the preliminary stage in the life of the Second
Republic. Between December 1931, and the outbreak of
the Civil War in July 1936, the regime was to pass through
three very distinct phases. The first of these lasted during
the years 1932 and 1933, and were marked by the adoption
on the part of the Government of a policy even further to
the Left, which, in its turn, began to result in a growing
Catholic, Conservative, and Royalist reaction. This period
was also characterized by the progressive disintegration of
the forces that had brought the Republic into existence; a
disintegration that was only temporarily arrested by the
alarm created by the attempted *pronunciamiento* of
General Sanjurjo in August 1932. The swing to the Right
first became noticeable at the local elections in the spring
of 1933, and was most pronounced in the general election
at the end of the same year. This state of affairs rendered
Azaña's position impossible, and he was succeeded by
Alejandro Lerroux. The second phase now began, and it
lasted until February 1936, and its chief characteristic was
a series of ephemeral Centre administrations, which, under
pressure from the Right, retraced some of the steps of
their more revolutionary predecessors. Finally, in February
1936, the third phase was ushered in by a general election
which revealed the real weakness of the Centre by comparison with the Right and Left: this period was marked

by a growing anarchy which finally degenerated into civil war in the summer of the same year.

Mistakes of Azaña

After making every allowance for the difficulties of his position it is not easy to reach any other conclusion than that Azaña's premiership was a disaster both for the Republic and for Spain. He settled nothing and he unsettled everything. He practised violence, forgetting that in politics violence begets violence. He was dependent upon the Socialists for support, and he did not hesitate to use all the machinery of the state against their enemies, both to Right and Left. The Communists and Anarchists rose in revolt in many parts of the country, and were suppressed only after some hard fighting, in which about a hundred people were killed. When he took office the Right was crushed; when he resigned it was a growing force. As for the Church, he acted in such a way that every practising Catholic was forced into opposition to the Government, if not to the regime. He had the chance of consolidating opinion in support of the Republic, but he behaved in such a manner as to prepare the way for civil war. As for the interests of the country as a whole, Azaña's stewardship is best illustrated by the fact that during the course of it the value of shares in first-class Spanish enterprises fell by 50 per cent, and that the export trade of Spain decreased by two-thirds.

The accession to power of Lerroux coincided with the rise on the Right of the Spanish phalanx, headed by José Antonio Primo de Rivera: it had branches all over Spain, and claimed 80,000 adherents in Madrid alone. Its strength in the new Cortes was thirty-seven, and this fact, taken in conjunction with the success of the Right as a whole, shook the faith of the Left in the parliamentary system: there was another Communist revolt, which in Asturias assumed the character of civil war in which there was considerable loss of life. Thereafter matters were allowed to drift until several members of the administration became involved in financial scandals, and Lerroux had to resign: meanwhile the parties of the Left were closing their ranks under the name of the Popular Front. In February 1936, recourse was had to new elections with a view to finding a way out of what had become a dead-lock, but they merely made the situation worse for the Centre was to all intents and purposes eliminated, and the two extremes of opinion were left face to face: nor were matters improved by the return of Azaña to the premiership.

By now Spain was relapsing into chaos. During the first four months of Popular Front rule 269 people were killed and 1,287 injured in political disturbances; 160 churches were completely destroyed and 231 partly damaged; 69 Right-wing political headquarters were wrecked and 312 were damaged; there had been 113 general and 228 partial strikes; while 10 newspaper offices had been sacked and 33 damaged.

Revolt of the Army in Morocco

In July the storm finally broke. On the 8th of that month Calvo Sotelo made a fierce attack on the Government in the Cortes, and as he sat down Dolores Ibarruri, better known as La Pasionaria, a Communist deputy, shouted at him, 'That is your last speech'. After that events moved rapidly. Four days later an officer of the Shock Police, by name Castillo, noted for his Communist sympathies, was murdered by Fascist gunmen outside his house in Madrid. At three o'clock on the following morning a detachment of the Shock Police came in uniform to the house of Calvo Sotelo, took him away, murdered him, and left his body at the gates of a cemetery. Another body visited the residence of Gil Robles, but he was already in hiding. The Government arrested the ninety men of the company to which Castillo had belonged, but did nothing more. On the 18th the army in Morocco revolted, and the Civil War had begun.

CHAPTER SEVEN

The Civil War and the Franco Regime

The struggle which began with the revolt of the Melilla garrison on 18 July had in its origin nothing to do with the clash between conflicting ideologies which was so prominent a feature of the contemporary international scene. The movement against the Government was at first purely military in its nature, and there were many precedents for it in the history of Spain. The revolting generals were thinking in terms of a *pronunciamiento* similar to that of Primo de Rivera thirteen years before, and it was only when their plans miscarried that they were forced to prepare for a civil war which had assuredly not entered into their original calculations. Certainly the movement was not monarchist in origin, for whatever the views of Franco himself, most of the generals, especially Queipo de Llano, had been strong Republicans at one time, and even Franco in the earlier days of the republic had refused to commit himself on the question of regime. Nor did the rising owe anything to the Spanish phalanx, for José Antonio Primo de Rivera had been arrested and imprisoned some months before it took place, so that he could hardly have been implicated. In fact, his fate was for long in doubt, and he was referred to by his followers as *El Ausente* — the absent one — until it was established that having been condemned to death by a people's court he was shot in Alicante prison in November 1936.

At the same time it is clear that the Nationalist blow forestalled one by the Communists. Documents which fell into the hands of Franco and his associates proved that the plans of the extreme Left were complete, and from them it would appear that the signal for a rising may well have been the murder of Calvo Sotelo: at any rate, very early in the programme occurs the ominous phrase, 'execution of those who figure on the black list'. Russian complicity, it may be added, was fully established.

Progress of the Revolt

However this may be, the original Nationalist plan was to paralyse the action of the Government by the seizure of all the more important centres of population at a single blow. General Franco, who was Captain-General of the Canaries, flew to Morocco, where he assumed command of the troops, with whom he was personally popular owing to his service there in the past. Even more remarkable was the exploit of Quiepo de Llano, who bluffed Seville into surrender at the head of 150 men: he first captured the radio station, from which he constantly sent out news that he was advancing on the city with an army of 40,000: he then put into lorries the handful of men he had, and sent them out again to various districts to create an impression of overwhelming strength. Elsewhere Mola obtained control of a large part of the north of Spain, while Cabanellas seized Zaragoza.

These were, indeed, considerable successes, but they were far from constituting final victory and they were counterbalanced by serious reverses. In the capital General Fanjul hesitated too long, and thus gave the Government time to arm the Workers' Unions, who overpowered him on 20 July, and stormed the barracks of La Montaña. Much the same happened in Catalonia, for General Goded, who commanded in the Balearic Islands, went to take charge of the rising, but was captured and shot. Finally, General Sanjurjo was killed in an air accident as he flew from Lisbon to join the Nationalists. Had he lived, he would have assumed the leadership of the movement, which now passed into the hands of Franco and Mola. Thus a few days after the first blows had been struck it had

become obvious that the rising had neither failed nor succeeded, and that a civil war, possibly of a protracted
nature, was inevitable. Such being the case, both sides
began to take stock of their position.

The Geographical Situation

Geographically they were curiously placed. The Government held Madrid, the whole eastern coast, La Mancha,
New Castille, and Estremadura. This cut the Nationalists in
the north off from those at Seville, but Guipuzcoa, Biscay
and Santander, which still acknowledged the Government,
were in their turn separated from the rest of the territory
under the control of Madrid. It is significant of what lay
ahead that in the main this had been the line of division
in previous civil conflicts. It had been so in the seventeenth
century when the Catalans accepted Louis XIII as their
ruler: it was the same again sixty years later when the
Archduke Charles held Catalonia and much of Aragón
against Philip V; and in the War of Independence the
Afrancesados were particularly strong in the east of Spain.
It was the old struggle of the Gothic-Celt-Iberians against
the men of Romance blood.

What may be described as the purely Spanish phase of
the Civil War ended in the first week of November 1936.
During this period power in Madrid shifted further to the
Left, and at the beginning of September the premiership
passed to Largo Caballero, and his Cabinet included men
of very extreme views. In the field and at sea the progress
of events favoured the Nationalists. Estremadura was
cleared of government troops, so that communication was
established with the Nationalists who were operating in
the north. The next step was the capure of Irun and San
Sebastian, thereby closing the western end of the Franco-
Spanish frontier, and so stopping the provision of supplies
to the enemy forces round Bilbao. Finally there was the
relief of the garrison of the Alcazar at Toledo. During these
months, too, the command of the sea passed from the
Government to the Nationalists, who were able to complete

the construction of some ships which were being built at Ferrol, and by the end of September the Government men-of-war, in which the crews had mostly murdered their officers anyhow, had suffered such losses that for all practical purposes they ceased to exist as an effective force.

Emergence of General Franco

On 1 November the Nationalists appointed Francisco Franco as Generalissimo of their armies and Head of the Spanish State for the duration of the war. At that time, although he was only forty-three years of age, he had a distinguished and varied career behind him. His father had been a naval officer, and Francisco was a second son. He had joined the infantry academy at Toledo in 1907, and five years later first saw service in Morocco. In 1920 he assisted Millán Astray in the formation of the Spanish Foreign Legion, and served with it until the end of the war, when at the age of thirty-three he was already a Brigadier-General. Franco's next appointment was that of commandant of the new military academy at Zaragoza, and he held the post when the monarchy fell. He served the Second Republic in several capacities as loyally as he had the preceding regime, saying that 'soldiers should stand aside from politics and think of the nation'. All the same he gradually came under suspicion as power at Madrid shifted to the Left, and he was virtually exiled to the Canary Islands, where he was Captain-General in the summer of 1936. The death of Sajurjo did much to bring Franco to the fore.

Intervention of Foreign Powers

As 1936 merged into 1937 foreign powers began to fish in Spain's troubled waters, and there was a real danger that, as at the beginning of the eighteenth century, a Spanish quarrel might develop into a European war. That this did not take place was largely due to the efforts of British diplomacy, but in spite of this, intervention there was, and Spain experienced, though happily only to a modified extent, the fate of Germany in the Thirty Years' War; that is to say she became the place where were tested the latest theories in strategy and politics.

France, Italy and Germany

One of the worst offenders was France, for the Popular Front administration in Paris naturally wished well to its co-religionists in Madrid, and it was stated in the Chamber of Deputies in December 1938, that between twenty and thirty thousand Frenchmen had gone to fight against the Nationalists. What finally caused the Popular Front government to change its policy was a realization of the fact that arms could not be spared for Spain in face of the rapid rearmament of Germany. Stalin's main aim was to keep the Spanish pot boiling without becoming too implicated: also, the Anarchist element, as opposed to the Communist, was too much to the fore for his liking. The greatest contribution to the Government cause was the International Brigade, recruited from Left sympathizers all over the world, though its exact strength is not easy to determine in the absence of reliable statistics. The official Nationalist figures put them at 100,000, but other observers estimated them at anything between 50,000 and 150,000. In any event they seemed to have been at least as numerous as the foreigners who fought for Franco. On the other side Germany and Italy recognized the Nationalist Government in November 1936, and thereafter reinforcements from those two countries arrived in not inconsiderable numbers, though there were never more than 46,000 Italians and 7,000 Germans, the latter being entirely airmen and technicians.

Nationalist Reverses

Thereafter the war continued with varying fortunes Franco had one great advantage over his opponents in that it was never necessary for him to guard his lines of communication, and so he was able to make the most

effective use of his man-power. All the same the Nationalists suffered two major reverses during the early weeks of
1937, for their drive on Madrid was halted by the International Brigade, and Franco's Italian allies, who were not
of high quality, were routed at Guadalajara.

As the war progressed it proved to be the most bitter
and the most bloody of all the civil wars ever fought in
the Peninsula. It was not that the fighting was at any time
on the scale which characterized the American Civil War,
but rather that, as the Nationalist forces advanced, the
evidence of the atrocities committed by the more extreme
supporters of the Government accumulated rapidly until
it amounted to a tale of horror which the outside world
long found it difficult to credit. Exact figures are impossible
to ascertain, but after the war was over it was officially
estimated that cases of murder amounted to 85,940, and
it is probable that the number of those slaughtered in cold
blood reached at least a quarter of a million. The Church
was a particularly heavy sufferer, and between fourteen
and sixteen thousand priests were murdered in the territory
controlled by the Government, while prisons were only
too often a synonym for torture-chambers. In these circumstances it is in no way surprising that the conduct of the
war in the field should also have deteriorated, and contemporaries, little knowing what was to be common
practice on both sides during the Second World War, were
particularly horrified at the bombing of the civilian
population from the air.

End of the Civil War

Gradually the Nationalist forces surged ahead, though
with occasional setbacks, carefully by-passing Madrid,
until at the end of 1938 they had 350,000 men in the field.
With these the main offensive was made in the east: losses
were heavy on both sides, but on 26 January 1939 Barcelona fell, and for all practical purposes the war was over,
though it still had two months to run, for it was not until
29 March 1939, that Madrid surrendered, and that date is

held to mark the end of the Civil War, in which it is estimated that over a million lives were lost. To their memory has been erected the gigantic cross in the Valle de Los Caídos.

Spain and the Second World War

Its termination gave Franco and his colleagues leisure to regard the international scene: they saw Europe divided into two armed camps, and events were to prove that an early clash between them was inevitable. Spain herself was utterly exhausted, and it was the primary task of her new rulers to take care that she did not become involved in any conflict which might break out. The difficulties were not inconsiderable. The Nationalists owed a great deal to the German and Italian dictators, and there was a strong body of Phalangist opinion which admired the existing order in Berlin and Rome; on the other hand, the Church, whose support meant much to Franco, regarded the Third Reich with disapproval and Fascism with suspicion, while the army and the monarchists could be relied upon to take a side opposed to the Phalangists in any dispute which might arise. Nor were the complications only of Spanish origin, for in two of the three wars of the previous centuries Spain had been a battlefield, so it behoved Franco to walk extremely warily if he was to avoid that false step which might so easily have completed the ruin of his country, worn out as she was by her long internal struggle.

The Part of General Franco

In the end he managed to keep Spain out of the Second World War, but to what extent this was due to his patriotism or his cynicism, to his ability or his luck, is likely to remain a matter of opinion. Certainly he was subject to a pressure which King Alfonso XIII had not known in its predecessor, and there was even a meeting between Franco and Hitler at Hendaye in October 1940, when the Führer sought the passage of German troops through Spain; but it was all to no purpose, and at the end of a lengthy discussion he summed the position up in the words. 'We shall get nothing out of that man', nor did he.

The Bourbons and the Future

Succeeding years have been devoted to the consolidation of the regime and the resurrection of Spain after her misfortunes of the previous generations. In 1942 Franco announced the revival of the Cortes, but in a different form: it was again re-organized by an Organic Law in 1966, and is now composed of approximately 564 members chosen from various organizations, heads of families and married women, representatives of local administrations etc. In 1967 the offices of Head of State and Head of Government were separated, but Franco for a time continued to hold both. Finally, looking to the future, in July 1969, he nominated Prince Juan Carlos of Bourbon, grandson of King Alfonso XIII, to succeed him as Head of State on his death or retirement, and this nomination was approved in the Cortes by a large majority.

CHAPTER EIGHT

The Spanish Genius

The influence of geography upon national character has never been better exemplified than in the case of Spain. An open country where nature seems omnipotent, with everything on a large scale, not unnaturally produces a nation of realists. The soil of Spain has not the richness of that of France; the landscape is by no means so varied as the Italian; and so the Spaniard differs very considerably from his fellow Latins. He is, as the record of his history abundantly proves, a realist, an individualist, and a good deal of a fatalist. He is capable of extraordinary energy, and some of the greatest feats in the annals of mankind have been performed by Spaniards; but he has not the taste for continued effort, and in the past he has rarely found the leader who can persuade him to undertake it. Yet, with all its drawbacks, the Spanish race has impressed Latin civilization (not only in a material sense) upon the greater part of the New World.

Individualism and realism

If individualism and realism are the most prominent characteristics of the life of Spain, they are also fully reflected in the mirror of that life, namely Spanish literature and art. Moreover, the continuity of the one is as marked as that of the other, and this in spite of vicissitudes to which no other west European nation has been subject. Martial joins hands with Quevedo, just as Viriathus was the prototype of the *guerrillero* of the war against Napoleon. Formalism is abhorrent to the Spanish genius, which is above all things interested in people rather than in abstract ideas, or mere literary and artistic conventions, as the pages of Lope de Vega and Cervantes, and the pictures of Velásquez and Goya, testify. It is true that in the early eighteenth century there was a determined attempt, inspired by the court, to imitate the classical example of France, but the only result was that the period is one of the most barren in Spanish literary and artistic annals. The Spaniard does not take kindly to foreign models, whether in literature or politics, and the eras when his rulers thrust them upon him are invariably jejune. He will consent to be guided by a foreigner, of whom he at once proceeds to make a good Spaniard, like Charles V or El Greco, but he revenges himself upon a foreign system by rendering it a farce.

In literature Spain has been fortunate in that Castillian early became the language of the State, for the *Siete Partidas* were issued in that dialect in preference to Aragonese or Galician. From that time Italian influence, notably that of Dante and Petrarch, was marked, but it was adapted, rather than adopted, and so served to reinforce the native talent. Satire was always prominent from Juan Ruiz to Cervantes and Quevedo; but, apart from the adventures of the immortal Don Quixote, Spanish literature of the golden age is best known abroad in the rhymed comedy of which the great masters were Lope de Vega, Tirso de Molina, and Calderón de la Barca. It is to be noted that all these dramatists portrayed life as they saw it, the life of the inn and the street, and it was not until the accession of the Bourbons that a change took place. The result was fatal, for the Spanish genius could not be moulded to the shape fashionable at Versailles. The national literature, like the national constitution, was too often a poor imitation of a foreign model, so that even the leading Spanish novelists of more recent times, such as Perez Gáldos, have not attained an international reputation. The best writers have been those who dealt with the life of certain localities, and that because they were less influenced by foreign schools of thought. The greatest Spanish poet of modern times was the *Nicaraguan*, Ruben Dario, so thoroughly has Spain done her work in the Americas.

Art

What is true of the literature of Spain also applies to her pictorial art. The prevailing tendency is to realism, though often combined with a naturalistic method of treatment as in the case of Salvador Dali, and it is no mere accident that Mazo is the only Spanish landscape painter of note. All those who have made the Spanish school so famous in the annals of art have concentrated in some form or another upon the individual, and this observation is applicable to El Greco, Velásquez, Murillo, Goya, and Zuloaga alike. Man, particularly man in society, in all his moods is what interests the Spanish artist, and this attitude remains unchanged down the ages, for such pictures as *Los Borrachos* of Velásquez are closely akin to the works of Goya. The humanity of the Spanish painter has, it must be admitted, often led to exaggeration and pomposity. There is a weakness for too much detail and an exuberance of material extravagance, which one finds also in many cathedrals in Spain. In literature this national failing attained its apogee in Góngora, whose style was so marked by affectation and mannerisms that the term Gongorism has ever since been used to describe this type of writing. In oratory, too, there is the same tendency to excess.

Religion

This absorption in man as man has not been without its influence upon the Spanish attitude towards religion, for the national individualism has made this a personal affair in a way unknown in France or Italy. The long wars against the Moors were not without their effect in making the Spaniard come to feel that God, as represented on earth by the Holy Catholic Church, needed the assistance of him personally, and that is why he supported such monarchs as Philip II in a policy of intervention in quarrels which were the concern of Catholicism, rather than of Spain. It is easy to sneer at the quixotry of a nation inspired with a crusading spirit, often to its own serious detriment for centuries, but there is something nobler about it than in the calculating selfishness that has only too often characterized the policy of, say, France and Prussia. One may regret that as the result of a hopeless struggle Spain was, temporarily at any rate, impoverished, with consequences that were detrimental to the interests of western civilization, yet it is impossible, even for the Protestant and the foreigner, to withhold his admiration for the spirit that prompted the attempt.

Moreover, it was this very exuberance, so ridiculous in some of its manifestations, that enabled the Spaniard to achieve what he did in the Americas, and his work there is perhaps his greatest claim upon the civilized world. Had he gone out in the same spirit as his English and French contemporaries he would soon have tired of the work, for the wealth which a few of the luckier *conquistadores* acquired was far from being commensurate with the sacrifices they and their comrades made, and the hardships they suffered. The vast majority of those who crossed the Atlantic from the Peninsula did so in the frame of mind of the Crusaders in the Middle Ages: if there was a chance of private gain so much the better, but the conquering of new kingdoms for Christ and his Church was the primary object.

Position of Madrid

Enough has been said to show that the Spaniard is fundamentally different from his French neighbour, and Madrid has never exercised the influence, cultural or political, of Paris, or, it may be added, of London. In most Spanish towns one is enveloped in the memories of some particular epoch in the country's history, such as the Ommeyad Caliphate at Cordova, or the earlier days of Castille at Burgos; but Madrid is not specifically identified with any historical event except the rising against Napoleon on

2 May 1808. It was raised by Charles V from the rank of a small town to that of the capital of a world-wide empire, and, save for a few years in the reign of Philip III, the capital it has since remained, although the empire has disappeared. Madrid was intended to be artificial, for it was the symbol of united Spain in much the same way as Canberra typifies the Commonwealth of Australia. Burgos would have alienated Aragón, just as Zaragoza would have outraged Castille, so a new capital was chosen which should not revive old animosities. Like Washington, with which many people compare it, Madrid is a capital and very little else.

The transitionness of its inhabitants is another prominent feature of the Spanish capital. Most of the people who live in London regard it as their home, but in Madrid this is very far from being the case; and in the upper and middle classes the vast majority are very definitely from Andalusia, or Galicia, or some other province. Provincial feeling exists in Spain to an extent which it is sometimes difficult for a foreigner, especially if he be an Englishman, to grasp, and the members of the highest aristocracy are not ashamed to speak with the accent of the district of which they are natives. Paris and London are so vast that they tend to reduce their inhabitants to a dead level of uniformity, but Madrid does not have the same effect, partly because it is so much smaller, but chiefly because the Spaniard is a far greater individualist than the modern Englishman or Frenchman. People flock to Madrid from all over Spain because it is the administrative centre, and a Government appointment is the goal of every Spaniard, but the number of real *Madrileños* is very limited.

It is the more astonishing that Madrid has exercised no great influence upon the course of Spanish history, for few cities pay so much homage to culture of all kinds. The University was founded at Alcalá by Cardinal Cisneros at the end of the fifteenth century, and was transferred to Madrid in 1837. Today it can bear comparison with any in Europe, and the University City is most impressive: a large number of the students come from Latin America. In addition to the University there are, as we have seen, numerous academies which deal with every aspect of human knowledge: in some ways these resemble the Royal Societies in England, except that the meetings are more frequent, and their proceedings are less technical in character.

Reaction against Imported Ideas

Finally, of recent years there has been a decided reaction against imported ideas, and not only in the political field, for in culture as well as in politics the Spaniard is beginning to wonder if he would not, after all, do better to seek his inspiration in his own country and traditions, and this tendency has received great encouragement from General Franco since his victory in the Civil War. There is a growing desire to return to all that made Spain glorious in the past, and by thus concentrating upon what they have in common to strengthen the bond beween the Peninsula and the nations of Latin America. Time alone will show whether there is to be a revival of the old Spanish culture along these lines, and it is certainly to be hoped that such will prove to be the case, for western civilization badly needs the strength that would accrue from a re-awakening of the rich genius of Spain.

Short Bibliography

Altamira y Crevea: *A History of Spanish Civilization*, London, 1930

Graham, Winston: *The Spanish Armadas*, London, 1972

Holt, E: *The Carlist Wars in Spain*, London 1967

Kamen, H: *The Spanish Inquisition*, London, 1965

Menéndez Pidal, R: *The Cid and His Spain*, London 1934

Merriman, R. B: *The Rise of the Spanish Empire in the Old World and the New*, New York, 1918

Petrie, Sir Charles: *Philip II of Spain*, London 1963

Petrie, Sir Charles: *Don John of Austria*, London, 1967

Petrie, Sir Charles: *King Charles III of Spain*, London, 1971

Petrie, Sir Charles: *King Alfonso XIII and His Age*, London, 1963

Robinson, R. A. H: *The Origins of Franco's Spain*, Newton Abbot, 1970

Thomas, H: *The Spanish Civil War*, London, 1961

Walsh, W. T: *Isabella of Spain*, London, 1931

Index

Abbasid, 25
Abd-el-Krim, 97
Abderrahman, 25
Academy of Fine Arts, 60
Academy of History, 60
Adrian VI, Pope, 38
Aix-la-Chapelle, Treaty of, 50
Alani, 20, 21
Alba, Duke of, 41, 42
Alberoni, 52
Albufera, 66
Alcántara, Order of, 28
Alcalá Zamora, 104, 106
Alfonso VI, of Castille, 26
Alfonso VIII, of Castille, 28
Alfonso X, of Castille, 29
Alfonso X, of Castille, 74
Alfonso, XII, 51, 78, 84–5, 87, 90
Alfonso, XIII, 90, 91, 92, 95, 96, 97, 99, 100, 101, 102, 103, 115
Algeciras Conference, 1906, 93
Algiers, 37
Almansur, 25
Almohades, 27
Almoravides, 27
Altamira: caves, 15
Amadeo, Duke of Aosta, 80–2
America: discovery, 10, 32; effect on economy, 33; English adventurers, 40; development, 53; independence, 71–3
American Independence, War of, 56
Anarchism, 92
Andalusia, 16, 40, 49
Anjou, Philip, Duke of, 51
Antonio, of Portugal, 41
Arab invasion, 23–9
Aragón, 26, 29, 30, 43, 49
Aranda, Count of, 57, 58
Architecture, 60
Armada, 39, 43
Armed forces, 35
Art, 9, 45–6, 60–1, 119,
Asturias, 18
Augustus, 18
Austrian Hapsburgs, 48, 51
Averroes, 29
Aviation, 98
Azaña, Manuel, 106–8
Aznar, Admiral, 100, 101, 102
'Azorin', 90

Badajoz, 67
Baetica, 18
Bailen, 63
Balearic Islands, 16

Ballesteros, 73
Balts, 21
Barbary Corsairs, 37, 40
Barbate, 23
Baroja, 90
Basle, Treaty of, 62
Basques, 85
Bavaria, Electress of, 50
Berbers, 24
Berenguer, General, 94, 100
Bermudez, Zea, 75
Bessières, Marshal, 63
Bolivar, 72
Bonaparte, Joseph, 62, 63, 65, 67, 80
Bonaparte, Napoleon, 62, 63, 65, 67
Bourbons, 52, 55
Braganza, Barbara of, 54
Brazil, 45
Brutus, D. Junius, 18

Cabrera, 75
Cacique, 87
Cadiz: Phoenician colony, 16
Calatrava, Order of, 28
Calderón de la Barca, 9, 45, 118
Calvo Sotelo, 98, 108, 110
Canalejas, 91, 92
Cánovas del Castillo, 84–5, 87, 88, 91
Caracalla, 18
Carlist War, first, 75
Carlist War, second, 84
Carlists, 77, 90; restoration of Alfonso XII, 85
Carlos, Don, 74, 75, 85
Cartagena, 16
Carthaginians, 16–17
Castelar, Emilio, 80, 83, 84
Castille, Council of, 33
Castille, 26, 29, 30, 36
Castillo, 108
Catalan, 16, 49, 98–9, 104
Cato, the elder, 17
Cave paintings, 15
Celtiberi, 16, 17
Celts, 15
Cervantes, 9, 46, 118
Cervera, Admiral, 89
Ceuta, 23
Charles I, 74
Charles II, 4–5, 49, 50, 51
Charles III, 55, 57, 59, 60, 61
Charles IV, 61, 62, 74
Charles V, 35, 36, 37–8

Charles VIII, of France, 34
Chile, 79
Christianity, 20
Chundaswinth, 23
Cid, the, 27
Cisneros, Cardinal, 33, 121
Civil War, 108–15
Columella, 20
Communism, 94
Compañia Telefónica Nacional, 98
Condé, 48
Conquistadores, 9, 10, 32
Constantinople, 30
Constitution: 1912, 68–9, 76; 1876, 86;
  military Directory, 94–100;
  elections, 101–2;
  First Republic, 82–4; Second Republic, 102
Córdoba, Gonsalvo de, 9, 35, 48
Cordova, 24
Cortes, 28–9, 33, 58, 67–8; 1876 Constitution, 86; closure, 96; elections, 105; revival, 116
Corunna, 66
Cristina, 75, 76, 78
Cromwell, Oliver, 45
Crusaders, 27, 28
Cuba, 72, 73, 87–8, 89
Cuidad Rodrigo, 67

Dato, 91, 93
Dewey, Admiral, 89
Dianium, 16
Diocletian, 20
Directory, military, 94–100
Domitian, 20
Don Quixote, 46
Dupont, General, 63

Ebro, 17
Economy: inflation, 33, 36
Education: primary schools, 52; reform, 91
Eight-hour day, 93
El Greco, 118
El Zanjón, Treaty of, 88
Elche, The Lady of, 16
Elizabeth I, of England, 39, 42
Emporion, 16
England, 40, 42, 43, 47; see also Great Britain
Ensenada, 54
Escorial, 44
España Sagrada, 60
Espartero, Marshal, 76

Family Compact, 54, 56
Fanjul, General, 110
Farnese, Elizabeth, 54

Ferdinand III, of Castille, 28
Ferdinand V, 30, 31, 34, 41, 45
Ferdinand VI, 54
Ferdinand VII, 64, 67, 68, 70, 72, 73, 74
Fernan Niñez, Conde de, 52
Ferrer, Francisco, 92
Figueras, President, 82
Fisher, H.A.L., 71
Flemings, 36
Flores, Father Enrique, 60
Florida, 56
Florida-Blanca, Count of, 58
France, 39–40; invasion of Italy, 34; defeat at Pavia, 37; frontiers, 43; battle of St. Quentin, 44; Peace of the Pyrenees, 49; Treaty of Nimwegen, 50; revolution, 53, 61; Family Compact, 53, 56; Treaty of Basel, 62; Spanish marriage crisis, 77–8; Moroccan campaign, 97; Spanish Civil War, 113, see also Bonaparte
Francis I, 37
Franks, 24–5
Franco, General, 52, 98, 109–16
Franco-Prussian War, 80
Franche Comté, 50
French Encyclopaedists, 58
French revolution, 53, 61

'Generation of 1898', 90
Germany: Spanish Civil War, 113
Gibbon, 24
Gibraltar, 51, 56, 83
Gil Robles, 105, 108
Goded, General, 110
Godoy, Manuel, 61, 62, 63
'Golden Century', 60
Government: Cortes, 28–9; power of the Crown, 33; centralization, 43, 59; *Juntas*, 67–8; see also Constitution and Civil War
Goya, 9, 118, 161
Granada, 27, 28, 31, 32, 40
Granja, La, 76
Great Britain, 50; Spanish Civil War, 113; see also England
Greeks, 16
Grimaldi, 56
Guadalhorce, Count of, 98
Guerrilleros, 64, 66

Habsburgs, 48, 51
Hamilcar, 17
Hannibal, 17
Harris, Phoebe, 58
Hasdrubal, 17
Hemeroscopion, 16
Henry, Prince of Portugal, 41

Henry IV, of France, 47
Hesiod, 15
Hidalgo, General, 81
Hispania Citerior, 18
Hispania Ulterior, 18

Ibarruri, Dolores, 108
Iberian tribes, 15, 16–17
Ice Age, 15
Indies, Council of, 33
Inquisition, 32, 33, 39, 58
Isabella I, 30, 31, 41, 45, 74
Isabella II, 75, 76–7, 78, 79, 80
Italy, 49, 53; French invasion, 34;
    French defeat at Pavia, 37;
    Spanish Civil War, 113
James I, of England, 47
Jesuits: expulsion, 57–8, 71
Jews, 29, 31, 32
John of Austria, Don, 40, 42
John V, of Portugal, 54
Joseph, King, 58
Jourdan, Marshal, 67
Juan Carlos of Bourbon, Prince of
    Spain, 116
Juana the Mad, 35, 41
Julian, 23
Julius Caesar, 18
Junta Apostólica, 73
Juntas, 67–8, 93
Justinian I, 22

Language, 29
Lannes, Marshal, 65
Largo Caballero, 111
Leon, 26, 29
Leopold of Hohenzollern, Prince, 80
Leopold I, 50, 51
Lepanto, 41
Lerma, Duke of, 47, 48
Lerroux, Alejandro, 106, 107
Liberals, 91
Literature, 9, 45–6, 60, 118; 'Gene-
    ration of 1898', 90
Lope de Vega, 9, 45, 118
Louis XIV, of France, 35, 45, 49, 50
Louis XV, of France, 53
Louis XVIII, of France, 73
Lucan, 20
Lusitania, 18

McKinley, President, 89
Madrid, 120
Magistrates, 19
Maine, 89
Malta, 40
Maria Cristina, 74, 90
Maria Luisa of Parma, 61
Marmont, Marshal, 67
Martel, Charles, 24–5

Martial, 20
Martinez Campos, General, 85, 88
Mary Tudor, 37
Masaniello, 49
Masséna, 66
Maura, Antonio, 88, 91, 92
Mendoza, Cardinal, 33
Merovingians, 22
Mexico, 78
Milan, Duchy of, 47
Military orders, 29
Minorca, 56
Mohammed II, 31
Mola, General, 110
Molina, Tirso, de, 45, 118
Monarchy: religious sanction, 58–9;
    succession, 74; restoration, 85;
    departure of Alfonso XIII, 102
Montesa, Order, of, 29
Montpensier, Duke of, 78
Moore, Sir John, 65
Moors: see Arabs
Moriscoes, 40
Morocco, 90, 93–4, 97
Mozarabs, 29
Municipal system: Roman, 19
Murcia, 16, 40
Murillo, 9, 46
Musa, 24

Naples, 30, 49
Napoleon: see Bonaparte
Narvaez, Marshal, 76
National Assembly, 99; first
    Republic, 82
National character, 117–21
Nationalists, 109–16
Navarre, 26, 29, 30
Navas de Tolosa, Las, 28
Nerpio: caves, 15
Netherlands, 36, 37, 39, 40, 42, 47,
    48, 49, 51
Nimwegen, Treaty of, 50
Numantia, 18

O'Donnell, Marshal, 76, 78
Olivares, Count Duke of, 47, 48
Ommeyad, dynasty, 24, 25
Organic Law, 1966, 116
Orleans, Duke of, 53

Paris, Treaty of, 56
Parma, 34
Parma, Duke of, 42, 53
Patiño, 52, 55
Paul, St., 20
Pavia: French defeat, 37
Pelayo, 26
Peninsular War, 64–6
Pérez, Antonio, 43

Perez, Gáldos, 118
Peru, 72, 79
Pétain, Marshal, 97
Philip II, 37–8, 40, 41, 44–5
Philip III, 45, 47
Philip IV, 43, 45, 47, 48, 49
Philip V, 52, 53, 54, 74
Philippines, 88, 89
Phoenicians, 16–17
Pi y Margall, 82, 83
Poitiers, 24
Pombal, Marquis of, 58
Pomponius, Mela, 20
Popular Front, 108
Populas, 19
Portugal, 18, 26, 41, 45, 57–8;
    Kingdom founded, 28, 29;
    independence, 48–9; Peninsular
    War, 66
Prado Gallery, 70
Pragmatic Sanction, 74–5
Prim, General, 80
Primo de Rivera, Miguel, 85, 94–100
Primo de Rivera, José Antonio, 105,
    107, 109
Pronunciamientos, 76, 79, 93, 94,
    96, 106
Puerto Rico, 72, 73, 87, 89
Punic War Second, 17, 18
Pyrenees, Peace of the, 49

Queipo de Llano, General, 109, 110
Quevedo, 46
Quintillian, 20

Railways, 98
Reccared I, King, 22
Reccaswinth, 23
Reformation, 35
Regency, Council of, 68–9
Republic: first, 82–4; second, 102
Requesens, 42
Ribera, 46
Richelieu, Cardinal, 48
Riego, 72–3
Riff, War in the, 93–4
Ripperdá, 52
Roads, 98
Rocroy, 48
Roderic, 23
Roman Catholic Church, 22,
    119–20; powers, 27; relations
    with the State, 38–9, 58–9, 91,
    107; *Junta Apostólica*, 73; anti-
    Clerical policy, 104–5; Civil War,
    114
Romans, 17–21, 22
Royal Spanish Academy, 60
Ruiz Zorrilla, 81, 82
Russia: invasion by Napoleon, 67

Sagasta, 86, 87
Saguntum, 17
St. Quentin, Battle of, 44
St. Vincent, Battle of, 62
Salamanca, 67
Salic Law, 74
Salmerón, 82, 83
Sanjurjo, General, 97, 106, 110
San Sebastian, Pact of, 103, 104
Santiago, Order of, 29
Santiago de Compostela, 25
Santo Domingo, 78
Sardinia, 30
Scipio Africanus, 18
Scylax, 15
Sebastian, King of Portugal, 41
Seneca, 20
Serrano, General Ramón, 84
Seven Years' War, 56
Shipping, 53
Shock Police, 108
Sicily, 30
Siete Partidas, 29, 74, 118
Silvestre, General, 94
Sixtus V, Pope, 38
*Sociedades Económicas de Amigos
    del Pais*, 52
Soult, Marshal, 65
'Spanish Marriages', 78
Spinola, 34
Squillacci, Marquis of, 56, 57
State, Council of, 33
Stone Age, 15
Succession, War of the Spanish, 51
Suchet, 66, 67
Sucre, General, 72
Suevi, 20
Sweden, 50

Talavera, 66
Tarik, 23
Tarraco, 18
Tarraconensis, 18
Taxation, 52, 55
Telephone service, 97
Theatre, 45–6
Thirty Years' War, 48
Tiberius Gracchus, 47
Toledo, 26
Topete, Admiral, 79
Trafalgar, Battle of, 62
Triple Alliance, 50
Tunis, 37
Turks, 30, 31, 37, 40

Unamuno, 90
United States, war with, 88–9, 91
Utrecht, Treaty of, 51, 53, 78

Valencia, 16, 27

Vandals, 20, 21
Vatican: Concordat, 59; *see also*
   Roman Catholic Church
Velazquez, 9, 46, 61, 118
Versailles, Treaty of, 56
Vespasian, 18
Victor, Marshal, 65
Victoria Eugénie of Battenburg,
   Princess, 92
Vienna, Congress of, 71
Villalar, 36
Villaverde, 91
Viriathus, 18
Visigoths, 21–3, 26

Vittoria, 67

Wall, 54, 56
Walloon Guards, 57
Wellington, Duke of, 64, 66, 67
Weyler, General, 88
William the Silent, 42
Witchcraft, 39
World War, First, 92–3
World War, Second, 115

Zaragoza, Archbishop of, 94
Zumalacarregui, 75
Zurbarán, 46